Assessing
Presidential
Effectiveness

A Guide for College & University Boards

Richard L. Morrill

AGB
PRESS

Assessing Presidential Effectiveness: A Guide for College and University Boards

Copyright © 2010 by AGB Press and the Association of Governing Boards of Universities and Colleges, 1133 20th St. N.W., Suite 300, Washington, D.C. 20036

Printed and bound in the United States of America.

Library of Congress Cataloging-in-Publication Data

Morrill, Richard L.

  Assessing presidential effectiveness : a guide for college and university governing boards / Richard L. Morrill.

      p. cm.

  Includes bibliographical references and index.

  ISBN 978-0-9792425-3-3 (alk. paper)

  1. College presidents—Rating of. 2. College trustees. 3. Universities and colleges—Administration. 4.
  Educational evaluation. I. Title.

  LB2341.M6375 2010

  378.1'11--dc22

                        2010004289

For more information on AGB Press publications or to order additional copies of this book, call 800/356-6317 or visit the AGB Web site at www.agb.org.

Table of Contents

Foreword

The process of conducting a regular assessment of a president's performance has been an accepted part of governance oversight for many years. The practice of a more intensive, or comprehensive, performance assessment of a chief executive's performance, conducted on a 3–5 year timeframe, has been long advocated by the Association of Governing Boards of Universities and Colleges (AGB). Some important and groundbreaking work on the subject has been published by AGB over the years.

In this new volume, the process of a comprehensive review of a president or chancellor's performance is given a fresh look by Richard Morrill, one of higher education's most thoughtful leaders. From personal experience in his presidencies to his study of the work of presidents and governing bodies, Dr. Morrill offers new insights in this sometimes overlooked process.

Drawing on past practice and linking it to current challenges confronting higher education and its governance, this latest work links presidential performance clearly to institution priorities, strategic plans, and academic and fiscal priorities. Today's higher education presidency is a constant mix of challenges that combines an expectation for exceptional executive leadership, academic innovation, fund-raising prowess, and a public profile. Added together it is a position with no "off button" and very little down time. In its totality, the presidency tells the story of an institution: a respect for its mission and history, and a vision of its possibilities that lie ahead.

Then comes the question: how is our president doing—not at a casual level, but at a level of depth that defines strategic success? In the end, a governing board's primary set of responsibilities is tightly interwoven with how well it addresses the presidency of its institution—selection, support and, when necessary, candid review and dismissal. The board needs to be committed to understanding its institution through the prism of a comprehensive presidential review.

Presidents don't succeed or fail in a vacuum; multiple internal and external forces and constituencies impact the overall performance of the institution's most central and visible leader. In addition to the comprehensive review, AGB encourages boards to periodically also conduct formal assessments of their own performance; the relationship between board and president, which AGB refers to as "Integral Leadership," can define a president's ability to lead aggressively and with confidence that the board is fully supportive.

Higher education is confronting new challenges as the country continues to look to its colleges and universities to ensure our global competitiveness. Ensuring effective leadership of our institutions is part of a board's responsibilities; Richard Morrill advances a practical set of principles and guidelines for your consideration.

Richard D. Legon
President

February, 2010

Preface

I begin with a confession. During the nearly 20 years that I served as a college president at three institutions during the 1980s and 1990s, presidential evaluation was neither high on my agenda, nor a burning issue for other presidents. In one presidency I had an episodic annual assessment for a few years, but I can't recall anything that came of it. Another time I was informed during contract renewal discussions that all the trustees and vice presidents had been polled, and that everyone except two board members expressed ready confidence in my leadership. There was no feedback about my achievements or shortcomings or methods of leadership, nor did I expect or ask for any. No reproach of others is intended about these circumstances because in those days the idea of evaluation brought to mind criticism and judgment. It made everyone uneasy, especially the president. While I enjoyed strong support and close ties with three different boards and their leaders, neither party assumed that formal evaluation was a necessary part of the relationship. I should have known better, but I expect that my experience was closer to the presidential norm than the exception.

I did, of course, receive informal feedback about my performance from vice presidents and deans and a few board members. Informal evaluation was, to be sure, going on all the time. After one rousing informal talk to alumni, one vice president whispered in my ear, "Great, but you have to talk more about athletics." Another time, early in my work at one institution, a highly distinguished and influential board member said over lunch, with others present, "I hear nothing but good things, but some people would like to see more of you." I changed methods and emphases several times because of comments and suggestions like these. At other times, though, I ignored, discounted, or didn't know what to make of the informal feedback, often out of resentment or stubbornness, especially if I didn't trust the source. My experience was a test case of the phenomenon that useful feedback on performance has a hard time making it to the top of the organization.

Over the past decade, a number of opportunities and experiences have allowed me to see much more attractive and even compelling possibilities for presidential evaluation and feedback. In retrospect, I see how I could have addressed some of the periodic frustrations of the presidency more adeptly, and how my work might have been both more satisfying and effective. In my role as a director of two corporations, for example, I have learned how companies try to embed a continuous focus on leadership development and succession into the practices and culture of the organization. The focus of feedback is on equipping people with the competencies they need to fulfill their responsibilities and develop their potential, not on making judgments or placing blame. New assignments and developmental tasks may focus on a variety of competencies, including the improvement of capacities in working with others, but the aim is to meet the larger goal of effectiveness within the organization. The evaluation of responsibilities and competencies is differentiated from the person, unlike what often happens in higher education.

I also have had the privilege of doing a good deal of research, teaching and writing over the last decade about leadership in higher education, especially at the Jepson School of Leadership Studies at the University of Richmond. These opportunities have given me confidence in the ways that contemporary concepts *about* leadership can enrich the practice and development *of* leadership. Some of those insights have been translated into my involvement in the work of the Association of Governing Boards of Universities and Colleges (AGB) as an author, presenter, and consultant over nearly a decade. Many of the ideas in two of my earlier books, *Strategic Leadership in Academic Affairs* and *Strategic Leadership*, resonate strongly with the themes that the Association has explored in its reports on the college presidency, especially *The Leadership Imperative*. One of the differentiating aspects of this current book is its focus on leadership as the touchstone for annual and especially periodic evaluation. In working with AGB on the design of a process for comprehensive periodic assessment, in co-developing a workshop on the topic, and in leading several comprehensive presidential and board reviews, I have had a chance to test the translation of ideas into practice.

This book grows out of these experiences, but its purpose it to situate the theory and the practice of presidential evaluation in a new landscape. It is the first AGB publication to focus systematically on periodic comprehensive presidential assessment as a separate process. As I shall argue, annual evaluation is a necessary prerequisite to periodic assessment, and serves the same purposes. Joint board and presidential assessment remains an important option and may be the form that periodic presidential assessment should take in various contexts and cycles. The practices in each case differ, but the principles remain the same.

This guidebook also places a larger focus on leadership development than do earlier AGB publications. That emphasis has been affirmed previously, but in this text it is illustrated more frequently, discussed as a motif in a proposed set of interview questions and is the topic for one section of the book. A premise of all AGB discussions of presidential evaluation is also that its focus cannot be limited to the president alone but must also include the board and other decision-making systems and relationships. This text agrees with that premise and draws on it in several contexts.

In a related insight, it becomes clear that a periodic evaluation of the president can become a decisive opportunity for the board itself to reach higher levels of performance. Presidential assessment provides the occasion for the board to deepen its understanding of the president and the organization, to connect and integrate elements of its own responsibilities, to intensify its engagement with the institution and to broaden its influence in shared leadership. An evaluation of the president takes the board inside each of the critical leverage points within the institution's trajectory of success. In evaluating critical performance areas like finance, fund-raising, and enrollment, and in reviewing critical processes like strategy and collegial decision-making, the board has the chance to gain an integrated view of the president's work as a central part of an integral leadership process. The board should come away from the evaluation with a sharper sense of its own agency in shaping the future by its support of the president's efforts to improve the work of the office and the institution.

> **The board should come away from the evaluation with a sharper sense of its own agency in shaping the future by its support of the president's efforts to improve the work of the office and the institution.**

The primary audiences for this book are board members and presidents, the staffs who support their work, and those who will take a leadership role in the evaluation process, including board chairs and external consultants. Others who participate in the evaluation process may also find it of interest, such as administrative and faculty leaders. Those interested in leadership in higher education and other types of organizations will find it relevant as well. As with other AGB publications of this type, the goals are to situate the issues in a contemporary context, to provide a conceptual framework for thinking about various approaches, and to offer practical and useful guidance. The book offers suggestions and illustrations for practice by providing questionnaires, policies, procedures, check-lists and forms, a number of which are found in two appendices to the book.

ACKNOWLEDGMENTS

My active involvement with AGB dates to the invitation that came from Tom Longin, then-vice president for research and programs, to write *Strategic Leadership in Academic Affairs*. Since then Tom and I have worked together on several AGB projects, including this one, and he deserves my deep thanks for his friendship and the enthusiastic encouragement that he has offered my work. Those early interactions with AGB brought me into contact with Rick Legon, now the energetic president of the association, who has spearheaded this project from the start. He has shown a quick and strong confidence in my work that often exceeds my own.

I am also especially thankful for the support of Merrill Schwartz, AGB's director of research, with whom I worked closely on an earlier revision of a major section of this book. Merrill is a true expert on presidential evaluation, and parts of Chapter III on Annual Assessment come from her publication for AGB on this topic. She has keen insights and is a supportive colleague. Because of consulting work that I have done for AGB that bears on this topic, I am very grateful for the support of Patti Kunkle, AGB's director of Board Education and Consulting Services, for her early involvement and cooperative support of this project. Her predecessor, Maya Kirkhope, first asked me to prepare a white paper for AGB on the topic, and her interest was vital in getting the ideas moving. I also have benefitted greatly from working with Kenneth "Buzz" Shaw, former chancellor of Syracuse University, in preparing and delivering AGB workshops on presidential assessment. Buzz is a joy to know and his superb knowledge of both the practice and theory of leadership in higher education has informed my thinking. Amanda Adolph, AGB's senior vice president for marketing and communications, has taken the lead in preparing the manuscript for publication. Her support, professionalism and clarity of thought have been invaluable and are much appreciated.

5

Chapter I

Presidential Assessment in a New Landscape

For the last several decades, American society has been captivated by the possibilities and the ambiguities of leadership. From tiny community service agencies to gigantic global corporations, from the White House to the schoolhouse, there is a lively interest in leadership and the complexity, even mystery that often surrounds it. Questions abound. Why do commentators so often lament the loss of great and durable leaders, even as popular literature celebrates success stories and leadership lessons that seem to be within everyone's reach? Are leaders born or made? If made, how is leadership taught, or better, learned? What exactly is leadership development, now a buzzword in most organizations, and how does it differ from management development? Do leadership attributes and competencies apply across organizational contexts, or are they unique to circumstance? Can leadership be assessed, and if so, by what criteria and methods?

Questions of this sort and many others are part of the contemporary landscape of higher education. Colleges and universities now offer hundreds of courses and programs that address the leadership theme in a variety of disciplinary and interdisciplinary contexts. Equally evident, colleges and universities are focusing ever more sharply on the development of the leadership capacities of their own personnel. Programs in management and leadership that focus on feedback, development and succession are becoming a staple of human resource offices, especially in larger institutions. Initiatives that have long been in place in the corporate world are increasingly in evidence on campus.

Given this context it should not be surprising that there is a rising expectation that the leadership of college presidents should be subject to regular and systematic evaluation. In fact, during the past two decades, presidential evaluation increasingly has become the norm in higher education. A survey on higher education governance conducted by AGB in 2008 shows that approximately 90 percent of those queried[1] conduct an annual assessment of presidential performance. Just a decade before, Merrill Schwartz found that only 50 percent of the responding private and 66 percent of the public institutions had developed policies on presidential assessment.[2] Undoubtedly, the figures mask a wide variety of practices and protocols in the formality and the effectiveness of the process. Nonetheless, for these reasons and those cited below, it is safe to assume that virtually every college or university now uses more or less systematic methods to evaluate presidential leadership annually.

Although widely practiced, the comprehensive periodic evaluation of the president involving an assessment every several years by both the governing board and a cross-section of faculty, staff, students and other stakeholders is less clearly in evidence. The 2008 AGB governance survey showed that 61 percent of private and 53 percent of public institutions use comprehensive assessment. One of the purposes of this text is to show the parallels, the relationships and the distinctions between annual and comprehensive assessment and, in particular, to highlight ways for governing boards to undertake periodic comprehensive reviews of presidential effectiveness

ACCOUNTABILITY AND PRESIDENTIAL ASSESSMENT

The widespread interest in leadership and its evaluation is undoubtedly one source for the growth in the evaluation of college presidents, and that influence takes several forms. My initial focus will be on the regulatory, administrative and social expectations for accountability in contemporary life, and its impact on the assessment of the work of chief executives in higher education. I shall take careful note in later sections of how new concepts of interactive leadership are shaping the theory and the practice of presidential evaluation. Yet, one perennial aspect of leadership has to do with the exercise of formal authority and the official powers of office, which in turn translates into a wide variety of legal and regulatory forms of accountability and compliance. Contemporary society is thick with regulation and expectations for documented processes of compliance.

> **The form and frequency of presidential evaluation are not defined, but in most cases boards and presidents have to answer for it and document its completion.**

Higher education is deeply and systematically regulated by every level and form of government. In public institutions, presidential evaluation may be entailed by statute or by the administrative requirements of central university offices or of state government. Regulation is not limited to government. The independent sector presses it own regulations and standards on higher education, especially through regional accreditation, and the specialized accrediting bodies in which most institutions have multiple memberships. The regional accreditors define presidential assessment as a responsibility of the governing board, or include it within their expectation that all administrative and educational programs must demonstrate how they measure their effectiveness. The form and frequency of presidential evaluation are not defined, but in most cases boards and presidents have to answer for it and document its completion. Expectations are set in other ways, too. Philanthropic foundations and national educational associations often develop and articulate "best practices" that then become tacit or explicit norms. Over time they are translated into criteria for grants and expectations of membership.

The trend toward documented accountability is propelled by many other regulatory authorities and influences, several of which have sharp teeth. Even though they differ greatly in the scope and intent of their requirements, they have shaped the new landscape for presidential evaluation. IRS regulations stipulate the need for systematic compensation practices for the "highly compensated" officers and others (above $100,000 for 2008) involved in the governance of tax-exempt organizations. The IRS generally expects governing boards to compare the chief executive's salary and benefits with leaders in a comparable group of institutions, and to make the decision deliberatively. As stated in the new IRS 990 Form for 2008, "Did the process for determining compensation of the (chief executive officer) include a review and approval by independent persons, comparability data, and contemporaneous substantiation of the deliberation and decision?" The questions do not require an affirmative reply, but a demur would likely lead to a review and more forms, questions and explanations. Although formal presidential evaluation is not explicitly required, a systematic approach to evaluation and compensation clearly satisfies the regulation and does so, as attorneys often put it, with "an abundance of caution." The IRS can levy "intermediate sanctions" of tax penalties against the president and members of the board for serious violations or manipulations of reasonable standards of decision-making. An egregious violation of IRS regulations would be a virtual "death sentence" since it could lead to the loss of tax exemption. These issues should rivet the attention of governing boards.

Many other political and legal realities are driving a broad and deep social concern for evaluation and transparency about all chief executive compensation. The Sarbanes-Oxley legislation for corporate governance requires CEO evaluation, and the Securities and Exchange Commission (SEC) mandates ever fuller disclosures and analyses in proxy statements about the basis and criteria for executive compensation. In the wake of the financial crisis of 2008-09 it is unmistakably clear that the government will control CEO compensation when federal loans or investments are in play, and will sponsor and/or encourage legislation that gives shareholders a formal say on executive compensation. Even when government does not act, proxy advisory firms recommend policies and the election of directors to enlarge the influence and serve the perceived interests of shareholders. Even though, again, these practices do not directly impact colleges and universities, they do so indirectly by contributing to a culture of compliance. Many members of governing boards are corporate executives or attorneys who live within these legal and regulatory frameworks. It is hard to expect college trustees to drop the concerns that are driving other sectors of economic and public life when they enter the campus boardroom.

Nor is it wise for presidents and trustees to ignore the congressional watchdogs who often pounce quickly to hold hearings or propose legislation on perceived abuses in the governance of charities and universities. Investigations and hearings have been held in the past several years on the compensation of college presidents, the accuracy of financial reporting on the use of federal research funds, and on university tuition pricing and endowment spending patterns. In surveying the political context for higher education, the 2009 AGB report *Strategic Imperatives* concludes: "Colleges and universities are likely to continue to see more attention to their work from elected officials."[3]

CRISES IN PRESIDENTIAL LEADERSHIP

Hardly a week passes without the higher education press or local and national media reporting on the forced resignation or the abrupt termination of a college president, frequently in a swirl of public controversy. In contentious cases like these, the media become another powerful form of influence, now including the blogosphere where there is instant, continuous and anonymous communication. Through the anonymity and accessibility of blogs, issues can be kept boiling for months and sharp, even defamatory, personal attacks can become standard fare. In hostile public controversies about presidents, the good name of the institution suffers, disaffection grows among alumni and friends, battle lines form on campus and future presidential searches may take shape under a cloud of doubt among potential candidates.

> **Hardly a week passes without the higher education press or local and national media reporting on the forced resignation or the abrupt termination of a college president, frequently in a swirl of public controversy.**

During the past several years, for instance, there have been intense and widely publicized controversies over the presidencies at America's two oldest institutions, Harvard University and the College of William and Mary. At American University in Washington, D.C., the results of an audit of the president's expense account led to a deep split within the board itself. Given the university's hometown, the issues also occasioned congressional hearings. One consequence of this and other public controversies was an intensified focus by the IRS on compensation in tax-exempt institutions, which has now taken form in the 2008 revisions to the 990 form. These and similar cases demonstrate the depths of divisiveness that may befall an institution when the president's leadership is the subject of intense conflict. The board itself may become sharply divided and unable to function effectively.

Though sometimes less dramatic than these public crises, boards also have to deal with cases in which a faculty or staff organization passes a vote of no-confidence in the president. The motives, circumstances and influence of no-confidence resolutions vary widely, but they represent a decisive test of the nature of the board's support and evaluation of the president.

Board Assessment Practices

Though not a general pattern, some of the high profile cases of termination and resignation reveal that a governing board's methods for evaluating and compensating the president have been flawed, confused or unsystematic. In one instance, a decision to provide the president with a new contract and higher level of compensation was made by the board chair and the compensation committee allegedly without the knowledge or approval of the whole board.[4] In one case of abrupt termination, the board publicly affirmed the president's work after a formal evaluation, only to terminate the appointment abruptly six months later.[5]

The review of cases of presidential resignation or termination and votes of no-confidence reveals the benefits of a carefully developed set of formal policies and practices concerning annual and periodic evaluation of the president. With a solid process in place, the governing board is in a much better position to anticipate problems in the president's leadership that may be emerging, and to assure the campus and other constituencies that systematic methods are in place to consider issues and problems. If it uses continuous processes of evaluation, the board will have more confidence in the decisions that it makes and the responses that it provides to the campus and the public.

> With a solid process in place, the governing board is in a much better position to anticipate problems in the president's leadership that may be emerging...

Most of the crises and challenges to presidential leadership turn on the president's methods of leadership and the expectations created by the organization's traditions and culture of decision-making. If the president were to receive clear and explicit feedback about these expectations early in the presidential term there is a realistic chance that it could make the difference in creating a productive presidency. At the first sign of a serious problem, it is important for the board to focus its annual and/or periodic evaluation processes on the issues and provide the president with the mentoring or leadership development opportunities that might be decisive in making improvements. Well before a crisis occurs, it could decide to initiate a comprehensive review that would give the board access to the opinions and the judgments of a cross-section of the campus community in a fair and systematic way. The board has access to many types of information about the president, including its own direct interactions, but it cannot know directly what happens in campus relationships to which it is not a party. In some cases, the evaluation will not be able to prevent the clash that is in the offing. Yet, the more the board knows, the more able it will be to transform the problem over time, or to deal with the president's departure deliberately, keeping everyone's dignity intact, and avoiding damage to the institution.

> **The board has access to many types of information about the president, including its own direct interactions, but it cannot know directly what happens in campus relationships to which it is not a party.**

For all the reasons that we have analyzed, it becomes unmistakably clear why the board's evaluation and support of the president's leadership and development have opened into a much wider window of opportunity and responsibility. An effective evaluation process contributes to the success of the president and the institution, and prevents damage to the office and the person holding it. In both private and public institutions, presidential assessment has come to be seen as one of the central aspects of board accountability. As we shall see in greater deatail, it is easy to understand why AGB, the organization that adresses the wider interests, needs and responsibilities of governing boards, now explicitly advocates both annual and periodic comprehensive presidential assessment.[6] It has become impossible both logically and practically to separate the board's axiomatic responsibility for appointment of the president from the support and evaluation of the president's work.

TRENDS IN PRESIDENTIAL ASSESSMENT: DOUBTS AND POSSIBILITIES

It is clear that documented presidential evaluation is advisable as a form of prudence and required as a norm of compliance in today's higher education. Equally obvious are other questions, which are not answered by expectations for accountability and compliance. It is no longer a matter of whether, but of how to evaluate the work of the president. Precisely how the process should be undertaken—by whom, when, using what methods, relying on what information, and to what end—is fraught with critical questions. Compliance in general sets procedural requirements and establishes basic rules, but it does not raise the aspirations or recognize the superior achievements of an individual or organization. A college's flawless accreditation report, for instance, does not mean that it exemplifies the highest level of academic achievement by students and faculty. Compliance can and often does become bureaucratic and mindless, as larger purpose gets lost in a maze of checked boxes, templates and flowcharts.

If presidential evaluation is to reach beyond compliance, it has to find the right theoretical framework and adopt a series of carefully defined practices that fit the special circumstances of institutions of higher learning. In doing so, its goal should be to contribute to the enlarged effectiveness of the president, the governing board and campus decision-making processes, and serve the wider strategic ends of the institution. Happily, new ideas about leadership and ways of conducting assessments have emerged in recent years, which set the stage for effective and rewarding approaches to presidential evaluation and professional development.

EVOLVING CONCEPTS AND PRACTICES

Much of the literature from the 1980s and 1990s is highly skeptical of the idea of formally evaluating a position as complex and ambiguous as the college presidency, especially in going outside the governing board to do so.[7] The doubts that various influential students of the topic such as Clark Kerr and James Fisher have registered over the years are consequential, and they provide worthwhile cautions that should help institutions to define careful methods and criteria of evaluation. Universities are inherently home to conflicting interests and priorities since each academic unit and program defines its needs as incomparably worthwhile, and as internal and external constituencies press for influence in the decision-making process. Most issues can easily and quickly become politicized on campus, in the public arena and in the press, especially in public and prominent institutions. When those circumstances arise, commentators suggest, the already fragile authority of the president can be undermined. Critics and politically motivated opponents will line up to take potshots that undercut the president's effectiveness. Even if undertaken with good will, poor systems and methods of evaluation can produce largely meaningless results or breach norms of confidentiality. It is argued that evaluations can do more harm than good in leadership and governance systems that are as collegial, delicate and complicated as those in a college or university. Nor is it not hard to find examples of what critics of presidential evaluation find objectionable. In some public institutions, the evaluation of university presidents includes quantitative performance rankings filled in by thousands of state residents. How opinion polls could ever be useful in either appraising or improving the president's effectiveness is hard to imagine.

> **Even if undertaken with good will, poor systems and methods of evaluation can produce largely meaningless results or breach norms of confidentiality.**

In considering and weighing these critiques and concerns, John Nason's 1980 AGB publication *Presidential Assessment* reflected an important point of transition in a gradual shift from idiosyncratic and informal to systematic and formal methods of presidential evaluation.[8] Nason was writing at a time when much of the literature and opinion on presidential evaluation were influenced by the campus tumult of the 1970s and reflected skepticism about the idea. He carefully tracks different points of view about both the possibilities and the risks of evaluation in a politically charged campus environment. Although he is eminently wise and cautious in reviewing both the *pros* and the *cons* of evaluation, Nason makes it quite clear that most institutions and their presidents will benefit from a formal policy of presidential evaluation. Given the enormous variety of institutions and their practices and circumstances, he does not recommend a single method or system. Instead he offers a variety of examples of principles, policies, and practices for both annual and systematic presidential assessment. Nason importantly suggests that presidential assessment is never just the evaluation of an individual, but connects directly to the governance systems of the institution, especially the work of the board.

> **Annual assessment is typically understood to be a board responsibility that does not involve direct participation by other constituencies.**

In 2001, AGB issued a useful booklet on annual presidential assessment. The author, Merrill Schwartz, completed doctoral research on the topic and recommends a series of principles and practices to define the various steps in presidential evaluation, especially annual assessment.[9] As we shall have a chance to review in some detail, the core of the process is a written self-assessment by the president that is then reviewed by the board or a board committee and discussed with the president. Annual assessment is typically understood to be a board responsibility that does not involve direct participation by other constituencies.

The issues and practices considered by Nason, Schwartz and others on the essential link between board and presidential assessment became the theme of an important 2000 AGB study and guidebook by Richard T. Ingram and William Weary. *Presidential and Board Assessment in Higher Education* expands systematically on the rationale and the protocols for a periodic joint evaluation of board and president, which they emphasize as the appropriate way to assess the work of the president. The book suggests that a joint presidential and board evaluation should supplement regular annual reviews of the president and occur roughly on a five-year cycle. It should include feedback and insight from a variety of constituencies including faculty, students, staff, alumni, and, as relevant, church leaders, legislators and public officials. The authors strongly emphasize that the assessment of presidential and board performance should be gathered primarily through interviews by an experienced higher education professional from outside the institution, based on questions that reflect the various aspects of the president's and the board's responsibilities and relationship. The use of quantitative questionnaires or rating forms is strongly discouraged because they will necessarily distort, trivialize and possibly politicize the complexity of the work of the president and the board. "They greatly oversimplify the human qualities, complex behaviors, and confluence of interactions with other individuals and situations by which human beings perceive other human beings."[10] The book is highly sensitive to the delicate balance of presidential and board responsibilities, and provides a variety of useful suggestions for protocols and methods that will produce constructive results for the president, board and institution.

The work and publications of AGB over the past three decades offer an excellent point of departure to consider the evolving theory and practice, pitfalls and possibilities of a comprehensive approach to presidential assessment. Such an approach would involve the perspectives not only of the governing board, but of staff, faculty, students, alumni and other stakeholders. The earlier AGB studies and its current reports and documents offer a framework within which to develop an additional form of presidential assessment. The model of periodic comprehensive assessment can join annual, and joint presidential and board assessment as an alternative that will be appropriate in many circumstances. The methods and emphases in the various forms of evaluation may differ, but many of the principles and protocols remain the same.

As will become clear, the basic purposes of annual and joint presidential and board assessment are the same as those to be proposed for comprehensive periodic assessment. The procedures and emphases in the various approaches complement one another. Effective periodic presidential assessment ideally builds on an annual process that includes a presidential self-assessment and a variety of strategic and operational goals. If recent self-assessments are not available—if, for example, they have been done orally or sporadically—a comprehensive periodic process lacks an adequate foundation. An evaluative framework will need to be created for the process, including a presidential self-assessment, and a series of goals, expectations and performance indicators.[11] In turn, comprehensive assessment draws on wider sources of information and judgment, so it is able to place a larger relative focus on leadership development. Further, every comprehensive presidential review will include a clear focus on the relationship between the board and president, as well as on other academic and administrative mechanisms of decision-making. It may well lead to the board's own self-assessment, or to a commitment to undertake a joint presidential and board review at a future date.

Integral Leadership

The Leadership Imperative, AGB's 2006 Report of the Task-Force on the State of the Presidency in American Higher Education, chaired by the honorable Gerald L. Baliles, former governor of Virginia, captures many of the evolving motifs concerning presidential assessment and board governance in the concept of integral leadership. Integral leadership connects the work of the president, administration, faculty, students, governing board and other constituencies into an active partnership devoted to fashioning a well-defined vision. It offers a constructive interpretation of the possibilities of shared governance that goes well beyond the differentiation of roles in decision-making. Deciding who has the power and prerogatives to do what, when, is necessary but not sufficient for understanding the possibilities of integral leadership. The report makes a telling conceptual shift by re-interpreting the concept of shared governance through the lens of shared leadership. Integral leadership describes a process and a set of active relationships, not just the rights and responsibilities that come with holding certain positions in an academic hierarchy. It involves shared leadership among the governance partners in crafting a strategic plan that sets an agenda for the future. The strategy recounts the organization's saga, its narrative of identity through time, and uses a variety of methods of shared decision-making and collaborative leadership to implement the university's mission and vision in a changing world. If strategy is about clarifying purpose, setting directions and establishing priorities driven by a vision, it has to be a form of leadership.

Integral leadership clearly depends on a variety of presidential powers and responsibilities, skills and relationships, practices and behaviors, and capacities and values, all of which are integrated into a larger organizational process of governance and leadership. The concept echoes many of the themes that one finds in contemporary accounts of relational leadership as an active partnership between leaders and participants. Unless someone is following, no one is leading. In describing what he calls *embedded* leadership, James MacGregor Burns, the dean of leadership scholars, suggests, "Instead of identifying individual actors simply as leaders or simply as followers, we see the whole process as a *system* in which the function of leadership is palpable and central but the actors move in and out of leaders and follower roles."[12]

For the first time in AGB's history of making recommendations for board policies and practices, the *Leadership Imperative* explicitly calls for the periodic comprehensive assessment of the president in a separate process. As the report puts it:

> "Evaluate a president's performance based on clearly defined, mutually agreed-upon performance goals. A board helps ensure the institution's continued vitality by conducting annual assessments and providing feedback on the president's performance. In addition, boards should conduct more comprehensive presidential evaluations every three to four years. These evaluations should be based in part on the quality of the executive leadership team as well as on the president's ability to engage the support of faculty and other stakeholders in defining and pursuing a strategic vision."[13]

AGB's 2006 "Statement of Accountability" makes a similar recommendation about the need for annual and periodic comprehensive assessment, as do its 2009 publications, *Effective Governing Boards: A Guide for Members of Governing Boards of Independent Colleges* and *Universities and Effective Governing Boards: A Guide for Members of Governing Boards of Public Colleges and Universities*. For all these reasons and others, the systematic evaluation of presidential leadership increasingly has become a norm of good practice for higher education governing boards. Going well beyond the requirements of compliance, it has become a method for the continuous improvement of the president's leadership, the board's engagement and the organization's performance.

Chapter II

Principles and Purposes: The Board's Responsibilities in Appraisal and Development

As we shall see in this chapter, the evaluation of presidential performance in all its forms depends on a series of basic concepts, principles and purposes. Every question or comment about presidential performance reflects hidden presuppositions and underlying criteria. They reflect expectations for the role, the assumed responsibilities of the position, and the attributed competencies and characteristics that leadership is understood to include. All these expectations have to be tested against the realities of leadership in academic communities. The evaluation of presidential leadership has to resonate as well with the specific mission and vision of each institution and what it means for the president and others to fulfill them.

THE CULTURE OF ACADEMIC DECISION-MAKING

Those who lead and participate in the evaluation process need to have a clear understanding of the way local factors and assumptions about leadership are shaped by the nature of presidential authority within the decision-making world of academe. Trustees and other respondents may have to bracket many of their ideas about authority and leadership derived from other contexts. Academic leadership is different and has to be understood on its own terms. The focus should not be narrowly on the president as a solitary individual but on the wider organizational and social context in which the president operates. In his still-valuable early study, John Nason argues in several contexts that the evaluation of the president is also an assessment of the state of the collegial decision-making system, and the performance of the board, the faculty, and staff among others.

> "The president acts within an institutional context which is deter-
> mined by the attitude of the faculty, the behavior of the student body,
> the presence or absence of collective bargaining, the influence of
> alumni, legislators and self-interest groups, the degree of control by
> the central office in a statewide system, and most critically the extent
> of authority and responsibility of the governing board. An adequate
> appraisal of the president's role *must* take into account the attitudes,
> prerogatives and behavior of these groups."[14]

To recognize these realities lightens the burden of a leadership evaluation on the president as a single individual. Moreover, it opens the door for more effective and creative perspectives on ways to connect improvement in the president's performance to improvement in the institution. This basic awareness will help us repeatedly to define the scope and purpose of presidential evaluation and the benefits and opportunities that it brings to the board in particular.

As we have noted, much of the literature on presidential evaluation is cautious or skeptical about the process because leadership is complex, and especially so in organizations like colleges and universities where autonomous academic professionals play the central roles. The system of academic authority is widely dispersed and highly decentralized. It necessarily depends on processes of peer judgment and collaborative decision-making that are based on professional expertise. Decisions on academic programs and faculty performance are made by departments, programs and committees that are largely self-governing. Administrators, including the president, are often attributed the responsibility for what happens in the academic sphere since it embodies the mission of the organization. Yet, presidents have little direct authority to determine what is taught by whom or how, what is made the subject of research, nor, depending on the size of the institution, who is appointed and given permanent positions on the faculty. The wheels of academe also grind slowly and finely, creating bewilderment among the trustees and impatience in the chief executive about the complexity of collaborative decision-making.

The system of academic authority is widely dispersed and highly decentralized.

A parallel system of decision-making operates in more hierarchical fashion in administrative matters, but collegial processes are expected to be used in areas, such as finances and facilities, that involve academic priorities. What presidential leadership and effectiveness should and can be in such a truncated system often bedevils governing boards, especially when change is required. As one authority on the presidency put it in AGB's 1996 report, *Renewing the Academic Presidency* "...university presidents operate from one of the most anemic power bases in any of the major institutions in American society...Academic presidents are like other chief executives in their responsibilities... But they are unlike others in the source of their authority."[15]

Even though the system may be frustrating, the board's appreciation and understanding of the values and culture of academic decision-making are prereq- uisites for an effective program of presidential evaluation. Aspects of the collegial model can be changed over time, but the first step in doing so is to understand how it works and the investment of self that academic professionals have in it. For them, collaborative decision-making embodies important values—like academic integrity, legitimacy and professional respect—that have ethical force. At its best, academic life is a calling that as Burton Clark reminds us, draws the self into "...a community of disciplined practice and sound judgment whose activity has meaning and value in itself, not just in the output or profit that results from it."[16]

25

Presidential Leadership

Another important principle concerns the need for the governing board to focus on what they understand by the term leadership itself. This is essential in both shaping the process of evaluation and in using the results to improve the performance of the president and the organization. Leadership is a many-sided phenomenon, as AGB's concept of integral leadership makes clear. Some of the central strands of presidential leadership relate to the responsible exercise of the formal authority of a position, others to successful organizational and personnel practices, many to competencies and expertise in decision-making, and yet others to personal behavior, values, and attributes that create trust and build confidence.

Although presidential authority is shared with others in the academic community, a college or a university chief executive nonetheless is also conveyed a wide set of responsibilities and powers by the governing board. Presidents, as we have seen, are accountable for an ever-expanding set of social expectations, laws and regulations, and for managerial, financial and personnel decisions that shape the institution's future. Though limited, the influence and authority of a president is real. The question often becomes not what authority presidents possess, but how they use what they have to set and implement an agenda for the future. By itself, the authority of a position can be reduced to the mechanical application of rules by a bureaucrat, or the petty tyrannies of a boss. Through interactive leadership, however, authority can be transformed into a resilient source of influence and motivation.

The Leadership Imperative joins other contemporary accounts to suggest that leadership is a process of reciprocal influence, and collaborative sense-making and direction-setting that occurs among leaders and the members and stakeholders of the organization.[17] In many ways, the authority, competencies and attributes of academic leaders are put to the test by their ability to mobilize the resources and motivate the members and supporters of the institution to create and enact a shared vision. As stated in *The Leadership Imperative*, "Integral leadership . . . succeeds in fulfilling multiple, disparate strands of executive responsibility and conceives of these responsibilities as parts of a coherent whole."[18]

The criteria by which the president is assessed should consciously reflect the various dimensions of leadership that the board and the president find most relevant and illuminating in advancing the work of the organization. As suggested in the *Leadership Imperative*, the characteristics of integral leadership include the effectiveness of organizational strategies and decision-making, the skill and cohesion of the leadership team, the ability to communicate the organizational story persuasively, and the capacity to develop a successful relationship with the board and effective connections with various constituencies. The president's ability to integrate these different facets and dimensions of leadership around a well-developed shared vision is one of the topics an evaluation should address.

In both annual and comprehensive reviews, the criteria for leadership should also be assessed with reference to the goals, expectations and metrics that have been established jointly by the president and the board. These will have been expressed in operational and strategic plans, prior annual presidential assessments, reports, memoranda and contracts. The goals and indicators will not have the same powerful simplicity as the financial bottom-line of a corporation. Nevertheless, they will define aspirations and provide measureable benchmarks that reflect presidential leadership and convey wider strategic possibilities for the organization. Both annual and comprehensive assessment provide the opportunity to assess goals and expectations from the past and to renew, reconfigure and create goals for the future.

THE RESPONSIBILITIES OF THE BOARD

The board's role in presidential evaluation is complex and subtle, so its purposes and practices have to be carefully defined. To start, there is an irony in the evaluation of chief executives by their governing boards. Although the board as a fiduciary body stands outside management, it is responsible for evaluating the work of the chief executive officer. Ordinarily, a governing board exercises oversight and only makes decisions and takes actions based on management's recommendations, but it acts directly in appointing, evaluating and compensating the president. In most managerial contexts, executives oversee the assessment, development and compensation of their subordinates based on direct observation of and participation with members of their leadership team in carrying out their joint and several responsibilities.

> **Although the board as a fiduciary body stands outside management, it is responsible for evaluating the work of the chief executive officer.**

Board members, on the other hand, especially in a collegial context, are not at the top of a managerial but of a fiduciary and legal hierarchy. How do they receive enough information and evidence to make decisions about executive performance? What is the validity, the accuracy and the reliability of what they know? What are their sources? Can the sources be trusted? These become central questions in the board's responsibility to evaluate the president.

Consider these characteristics of the board's circumstances and its access to information about performance. Most board members interact directly with the president each year in a number of lengthy board and committee meetings and in several social events. If they are board leaders, live in the college community, or have taken on a special assignment, they will see much more of the president. Trustees also receive a great deal of written information in reports, plans, budgets and board materials, and many interact frequently with the president by phone, e-mail, Web sites and mail. As a result, all board members have some direct point of reference for assessing the president's work, and others do so based on a reasonably broad set of interactions.

Indirect information also comes to board members through the comments and opinions of those who work with the president directly, including other members of the board. Even without asking, board members often learn a lot about a president's effectiveness from what faculty and staff members and various constituencies say, or fail to say, about developments on campus. Then, there are the commentaries that supporters or critics of the president offer to influence a board member's views. Trustees should know when they are being "worked," and change the subject if it is inappropriate, or filter what they hear.

> **Trustees should know when they are being "worked," and change the subject if it is inappropriate, or filter what they hear.**

In sum, most board members' base of information for making an assessment of the president's effectiveness is relevant and useful, but not sufficiently detailed by itself to perform a thorough review of executive performance and development. Reflecting these realities, the board's evaluation of the president in the past often has been informal and unsystematic and has fallen to two or three trustees who interact most with the president, one of whom usually has been the chair of the board.

Principles for the Board's Responsibilities

It is against this backdrop that the purposes, policies and practices of annual and comprehensive assessment take on special significance. The board in each case has special responsibilities since it cannot rely simply on itself as a source of information and judgment. It has to find the best available information about the performance and goals of the chief executive, and to supplement and enlarge its direct sources of knowledge. For these reasons, the board relies on the president's self-assessment and other relevant facts and opinion for annual evaluations, and on a cross-section of campus and community judgment in comprehensive assessment.

In working with the information that it receives, the board should rely on a *set of principles* to carry out a variety of critical tasks. The board *frames* its work in terms of its proper responsibilities and powers, and the limits of what it knows directly. It *tests* what it learns from the president and the campus community against its direct knowledge, insights and experience, and it *integrates* its judgments about performance with the information and metrics that it has about the university's strategic position. The board *decides* what actions it might take to recognize, renew or improve the president's work, and to address problems and opportunities in its own responsibilities or within the institution. In its fiduciary role, it also seeks to *guarantee* the substantive and procedural fairness of evaluation processes and protect them from distortion or arbitrariness.

In annual and comprehensive assessment, the governing board acts directly but within the framework of its knowledge, responsibilities and fiduciary duties of decision-making and active oversight. The evaluation of the president is one of the critical means at the board's disposal to give form to its own effectiveness in *defining, monitoring, evaluating,* and *assuring accountability* for the mission and *improving* the quality of the institution that it serves. A task that it may at first approach with diffidence can become a way for the board to be engaged in integral leadership without being intrusive and sliding into the role of management. In exercising one of its primary responsibilities, the board can find ways to renew and energize its own work and sense of purpose and to reach toward a higher level of performance.

PURPOSES

When set in this context, it becomes clear that both annual and comprehensive presidential evaluations fulfill a basic board responsibility and serve a variety of purposes and goals, and include a set of tasks that will increase its own effectiveness, including the following:

- Along with the appointment and support of the president, the evaluation of the president is a basic board responsibility.
- Assessment provides an appraisal of the president's leadership within the larger goal of contributing to the development of the president's effectiveness and the institution's success.
- It deepens the communication and relationship between the board and president, and makes the board's expectations explicit.
- Assessment deepens the president's self-understanding, and enlarges the president's and the board's awareness of the president's impact on others.
- It expands the board's knowledge of the work of the president and provides a powerful form of monitoring the institution's progress in meeting its strategic goals, which in turn renews the board's sense of engagement and purposefulness.
- Regular and documented presidential assessment fulfills the requirements for institutional accreditation and satisfies regulations and expectations for accountability.
- It synthesizes important institutional documents, statements and commitments, and contributes to the continuing work of strategic and integral leadership by anticipating emerging issues.
- It provides the board with insights concerning the effectiveness of the institution's methods of governance and systems of decision-making,

including its own, and thereby contributes to the board's goal of high performance.

- Evaluation demonstrates the board's and the president's commitment to the assessment and development of talent at all levels of the organization.
- Although not its primary purpose, assessment provides the governing board with relevant information useful in compensation decisions.
- The process affords the opportunity for the president and the board to consider the effectiveness of the president's service, actions that might strengthen it, how long both parties believe it should continue, and the steps to be followed should it be drawing to a close.

> **The ultimate purpose of presidential reviews is to contribute to the development of leadership effectiveness, which in itself includes various dimensions and facets of a complex process.**

APPRAISAL AND DEVELOPMENT

This list makes it clear that evaluation has several purposes that can be distinguished and sometimes separated in both emphasis and in time. The ultimate purpose of presidential reviews is to contribute to the development of leadership effectiveness, which in itself includes various dimensions and facets of a complex process. On closer examination, however, there is the sometimes vexing question of how the appraisal of performance relates to the development of leadership. Appraisal typically focuses on quite specific achievements or failures, on goals met or otherwise, and on past actions taken or avoided. Evaluation of both achievements and failures is essential for several reasons. The achievement of goals deserves recognition and rewards, and it provides motivation and confidence for people to aspire to yet-higher levels of accomplishment. Success quite literally breeds success and can create a momentum of achievement that penetrates the culture of a college or university. Initiative and leadership can then take hold at every level of the organization through the credibility of achievement. One of the tasks of top executive leadership is to translate accomplishments into momentum that sustains itself.

But failures, too, can offer deep lessons for leadership, and can contribute substantially to the future success of both individuals and organizations. The lessons of failure have to be diagnosed without blame and fault-finding to reveal analytically and dispassionately what went wrong and why. The point is to learn from mistakes and failures by confronting the "brutal facts" of a problem and by encouraging people to debate them openly in a search for the answers. In his modern classic, *Good to Great*, Jim Collins puts it this way: "Yes leadership is about vision. But leadership is equally about creating a climate where the truth is heard and the brutal facts confronted."[19]

These factors make it clear why the tasks of appraisal are necessary but not sufficient aspects of the assessment of presidential leadership. They need to be tied to a focus on development that is forward–looking and that charts a set of possibilities to improve performance. Logically it is hard to imagine how development can be real or concrete without some exploration of what has happened and why, what has been accomplished or not. What differentiates evaluation as development is the purpose of the process, and the focus that it gives to future actions and possibilities. The point is to learn from the past to prepare for the future. A person's natural inclination to want always to do better should motivate the process of development. This transforms what can be a threatening or ego-centered form of appraisal into a positive opportunity for improvement. Problems and weaknesses are recognized in terms of their bearing on strengths and the development of capacities, which is motivational rather than discouraging, affirmative rather than negative.

FAULT-FINDING AND PRAISE-GIVING

The difference between appraisal and development often turns on the attitudes that people carry with them to the process of evaluation. To be sure, the notion of evaluation calls to mind rankings and scorecards, and some people will bring a judgmental rather than developmental attitude. Everyone gets anxious about assessments of performance, including college presidents. Board members or other participants may harbor resentments towards the president, or they may have personal agendas that distort their judgment. Even more likely, they may bring a strong friendship with the president into the process. Board members sometimes dismiss criticism because it creates potential complications for them, either leading to their personal discomfort or producing a drain on their time and energy if the problem is serious. In these circumstances, a few board members may turn appraisal into fault-finding or praise-giving with both negative and positive evaluations becoming a pretext for other motives. When this occurs, each negative finding becomes a way to lay blame and show failings, and positive results a way to defend against criticisms. Either way, defenses are raised and motivation to change and improve is lowered for those being evaluated. Neither criticism nor praise by itself describes a path forward: an issue to address, a process to improve, a goal to set or a talent to develop.

An actual but disguised case will help to make these points in relation to fault-finding. A third-year president in an 8,000-student public university located in a mid-sized city in the Midwest received highly positive evaluations from most members of the campus community, including board members, faculty, students and staff, in a comprehensive assessment. Local community and alumni leaders were also positive. Two members of a 14-person board were, however, quite unhappy with their role in decision-making, which they believed should involve more direct and independent interaction by board members with campus groups in the name of accountability. This was a point of tension with the president, who saw random board member interactions with the campus to be a bad practice and precedent, and a form of board intrusion.

> **Neither criticism nor praise by itself describes a path forward: an issue to address, a process to improve, a goal to set or a talent to develop.**

Those same board members faulted the president in the assessment for not being more active in developing fund-raising relationships in the metropolitan area. They had made suggestions to the president which in their view she had not adequately exploited. For them, this in itself counted strongly against the renewal of the president's appointment, even after they heard the strong support that the president enjoyed across campus. The fact that the president did not make enough fund-raising calls became part of a small bill of particulars to criticize performance. There were no accompanying suggestions from these members about how the board should expect new plans and goals from the president to address the problem. Nor did they offer any ideas about ways the board might expand its own involvement in the process. There were no proposals for actions the president could take to develop her talents and expertise in this area. Although human motivations are not reducible to single explanations, in this case it appears that the fault-finding was a pretext for other resentments and conflicts. Based on this case, board members and leaders might ask themselves how they would deal with either negative or positive appraisals that show signs of being a pretext for other motives.

There are, of course, no fail-safe ways for the evaluation process to ban fault-finding or defensive praise. Nonetheless, a place to start is with the board's conscious commitment to the purposes of developmental assessment in support of the effectiveness of the president and the success of the institution. Board members assume a formal responsibility to serve the best interests of the institution and to discharge a crucial fiduciary responsibility. Trustees who let personal interests or pretexts determine their evaluation of a university leader fall short of fulfilling the responsibilities they have accepted. It is not unlike a judge who decides a case based on personal preferences rather than the law. In doing so, trustees forego invaluable opportunities to learn from the information they have received to develop the capacities and effectiveness of the president. "The primary purpose of evaluating the president's performance should be to improve it, not to assemble a record of faults."[20]

The purposes that we have defined also suggest that some decisions related to the president's performance may involve a variety of sources of information and require several steps and stages. It is not the purpose of presidential evaluation, for example, to set the president's compensation, but what is learned through the process often will have a clear bearing on those decisions, as we shall note in a subsequent section.

It is clear from these purposes and principles that both annual and periodic assessment should be inscribed in an understanding of presidential leadership as a many-sided task that goes well beyond the personality or performance of a single individual. In enacting these purposes, the governing board deepens its understanding of the inner workings of campus leadership, and of the state of the organization. It sharpens its own sense of mission, and increases its influence in legitimate ways. If one of the goals of the process is to foster integral leadership, then the criteria and procedures of the evaluation must reflect that perspective. The process then becomes a form of learning through feedback and development. It should result in plans and actions by the president and the board to improve performance and strengthen the presidency and the institution.

Chapter III

Annual Assessment

A nnual presidential reviews provide the foundation for all forms of presidential assessment. They embody one dimension of the board's basic responsibility to guide and support the chief executive. They do so by continuously clarifying the board's expectations concerning presidential performance and priorities, and by enabling the board to be well informed about the president's effectiveness. They provide as well a record of the president's and the board's evolving conversations about performance, and an ongoing evaluation of the goals and indicators that the president has targeted for achievement. Without a basis of goals and findings in annual assessments, those conducting comprehensive reviews will have a difficult time finding an informed point of departure and getting traction for the process. Comprehensive evaluation in turn enlarges the board's sources of information about the president's work, and gives the board and the president a wider set of insights about ways to continue to improve the president's performance.

By convention in the literature of AGB and by usage in the policies of higher education over the past couple of decades, presidential assessments have been divided into the categories of annual and comprehensive. Although the basic purposes are the same, the distinction between the two consists in the frequency, emphases, duration, sources, and criteria for evaluation.[21] Unlike annual reviews, comprehensive evaluations take place every three to four years. Whereas the annual process should require a month or so to complete, comprehensive reviews will take up to four months. Perhaps most importantly, a comprehensive review involves evaluations from a variety of participants at different levels of the organization, while annual reviews typically are limited primarily to the board's and the president's perspectives. Although they use many of the same criteria of performance, a comprehensive evaluation explores a larger set of contexts and sources more systematically and deeply. As a consequence, a comprehensive assessment also lends itself to a fuller exploration of possibilities for leadership development. We shall explore these differences both in this and the subsequent chapter on comprehensive assessment. In this context we shall analyze three broad issues concerning annual evaluation: (1) board policies, (2) presidential self-assessment, and (3) board practices.

Board Policies

As AGB survey data have shown, the performance of most college and university chief executives is evaluated annually by their governing boards, or by a designated board committee. To set the process in motion, evaluation should be contemplated and enabled at the time of appointment. The initial contract or letter of appointment should define goals and expectations and include reference to accompanying board policies on presidential evaluation. (See *Appendix I, Section A* for a sample policy statement.) The analyses of institutional strategic position and aspiration that are often developed as part of the search process also can be invaluable in defining the broad issues with which a new president will be expected to deal. New presidents enter an organizational world that is filled with unknown expectations for their leadership, defined both by local tradition and convention and by people's hopes and dreams. The board can play an invaluable role in helping to define both orally and in writing some of those expectations and the process by which the president's efforts will be evaluated both annually and comprehensively.

ROLE OF THE ASSESSMENT COMMITTEE

The governing board should develop clear policies and procedures concerning which board or committee members will undertake the annual evaluation, and the authority they have to do so. The differences in board size and composition, in mission and traditions of governance, and in private or public sponsorship will heavily influence the policies and practices in this regard. Large boards will undoubtedly delegate the responsibility for the assessment to the personnel, compensation or executive committee. Small boards may choose to take on the task themselves, though in many cases the chair asks a committee to lead the process.

One of the critical issues for the committee is to decide what information other board members will receive and how they will be involved in the process. These questions become especially important if disagreements or controversies arise. Then a lack of clarity can be a source of confusion and contention. The assessment committee and/or its chair (typically the chair of the board) will necessarily take the lead in discussing performance and compensation with the president, but the board itself needs to be fully informed about both the process and the results of the review, and expectations concerning confidentiality

ROLE OF THE BOARD CHAIR

In most cases, the chair of the board will be a central actor in the evaluation process. But, again, there should a clear understanding of the role, responsibility and authority of the chair. Collegiate board member sometimes operate with inapt hierarchical assumptions about the authority of a collegiate board chair based on their familiarity with chief executive and chair authority in the corporate world. As a result, it sometimes falls to the chair working almost alone to make the most important decisions about the president's performance, compensation and even retention. Some of the cases that have gained the national limelight for questionable presidential compensation practices arose out of situations in which the board's chair and several other trustees made major contractual and compensation decisions of which other board members were not aware. This pattern of decision-making flies in the face of the fundamental norm that boards exercise their authority collectively, and that no single individual can speak or act for the whole without explicit delegated authority to do so. The chair is the first among equals in collegial forms of governance, and is not an executive.

> **The chair is the first among equals in collegial forms of governance, and is not an executive.**

Fundamental decisions on the appointment, evaluation, retention and compensation of the president are shared and should be carried out according to carefully described and understood protocols and policies. Although shared decision-making does not follow a single pattern, the actions of committees and board leaders relating to presidential evaluation must be consistent with the powers of the board as defined in its charter, by-laws and policies.

CONFIDENTIALITY

For good reasons that are widely understood and honored throughout society, personnel evaluations should be confidential. Confidentiality protects a series of fundamental values that are based on respect for persons and their rights, interests and privacy. It preserves an individual's good name and reputation and the potential harm that can come from *ad hominem* criticism or slanted or erroneous reports about performance. Laws against slander and defamation are designed to protect against unwarranted and vicious public statements that damage a person's rights and interests without due process of law.

Although assessments of performance take place in a special context, there are times when the unauthorized release of private information could be libelous or defamatory. To be sure, presidents carry out public functions, even in private institutions, so public criticism and negative commentary come with the territory. Indeed, some states even hold public hearings to evaluate a president's performance. That is a political and legal matter and, while it may comport with some open meeting and record laws, it does not define good executive development practices. Presidents will inevitably have critics and constituencies who have negative opinions about their decisions and performance, and sometimes the criticism becomes severe. But the details of the criticism and its sources should never be made public through the process of evaluation. To guarantee fairness to the individual and to those who have provided evaluations, the process must be methodical, balanced and private.

> **...confidentiality is essential if the board is to receive full and frank opinions from its own members and participants in the campus community.**

Although often less relevant for many forms of the annual evaluation of the president, it becomes especially clear in comprehensive assessment that confidentiality is essential if the board is to receive full and frank opinions from its own members and participants in the campus community. If sources of information or opinion were to be known by the president, many would feel reluctant to offer critiques that might be seen as leading to some form of direct or indirect sanction. On the other hand, many would see positive comments as a way to curry favor with the president.

Individual board members also have to be counted on to keep their opinions and deliberations about the president's work to themselves, and board leaders need to remind all members continually of this fiduciary responsibility. One of the basic duties of a trustee is to maintain silence outside the boardroom on personnel matters, whatever may be said within it. Unhappily, there are times when trustees reveal far too much to friends and associates on and off the campus about the president's evaluation, especially when controversies or deep differences of opinion divide the board itself. Few things are worse for the board and the institution than for bitter divisions in the board to spill into the press or across campus. The damage that is done to the institution's prospects and support can be telling and lasting.

> ...there is every good reason for the board to share widely, pro-actively and transparently the process that it uses to evaluate the president's work both annually and periodically.

On the other hand, there is every good reason for the board to share widely, pro-actively and transparently the process that it uses to evaluate the president's work both annually and periodically. The process is not secretive, but based on procedures, information, reports and deliberations the form of which the public and the campus are entitled to know. Presidents and boards themselves also may and often do decide to reveal to the campus, and hence the public, some of the general conclusions of the annual and/or periodic evaluations, and the priorities that the president and the board have established for the future. This can be done in dignified and appropriate ways, especially since much of the work of assessment focuses not on the president alone, but on the work of the organization and the board itself.

In many states, public institutions must conduct the formal deliberations and actions related to presidential reappointment and compensation in open meetings, though detailed deliberations on personnel matters ordinarily can be discussed privately. In some states, sunshine and open-records laws extend to all the written information that comes to the board concerning presidential performance, and in others even the formal deliberations by the board about performance leading to a decision are supposed to be in open session.

In general, of course, this means that the governing boards in these states exercise a high degree of caution and diligence about how and when they review written materials, and the ways and the contexts in which they discuss performance. They seek to follow state law scrupulously while having neither a detailed public discussion of the sources for their judgments nor an open discussion of the specific achievements and failures, and strengths and weaknesses, of the president and other top personnel. Since state laws are constantly changing, often in response to a scandal or high-profile problem, boards have to exercise diligence in responding to changing expectations and in obtaining the best legal advice about their responsibilities.

Presidential Self-Assessment

As we have noted, college presidents sit atop a complex organization with a decentralized system of decision-making that includes multiple programs and constituencies pursuing their own interests. Presidents sometimes feel that they are the only ones on campus with a full understanding and consistent commitment to the good of the whole enterprise. In the minds of many presidents and boards, these realities do not augur well for a fair process of evaluation. Presidents are often anxious that they will have little or no influence over the evaluation, and boards sometimes fear that they will lose control to determined individuals and groups pursuing an agenda. Because of these factors, some boards and presidents continue to resist evaluation, seeing it as unnecessary, awkward or a waste of time.[22]

A 1997 survey of academic presidents and board chairs by AGB sheds a different light on the issue. Most presidents found their reviews helpful, and less than 5 percent reported any negative results. Citing a 1991 study from business by Longenecker and Gioia, with which university presidents would resonate, Merrill Schwartz notes, "Paradoxically, the study found that the higher one climbs on the corporate ladder, the more evaluation practices deteriorate. Those at the top, literally without peers, had the greatest problem receiving performance feedback, and they benefited from systematic review"[23] by a board.

One young president who pressed his board for a comprehensive evaluation explained to the author that feedback is invaluable to a president, especially given its scarcity for chief executives. He noted that conversations about the president's effectiveness are going on all the time anyway, both within the board and among faculty and staff, and it is important for the president to tap into those exchanges. Assessment is a way for the president to learn what's going well and not so well and to have a basis to respond to those perceptions. The president also emphasized that evaluation at the president's level serves as a powerful model for everyone else on campus.

> In most programs of leadership development, self-awareness is the most important element, since it continually funds the process of improvement.

One of the most effective ways to engage the president in the annual review process is to build it around the president's own self-assessment. This approach also builds trust between the president and board, and binds them together in a cooperative relationship.[24] Most importantly, a self-assessment gives the president a chance to step back from the unrelenting press of events to gain some personal distance, and to deepen self-awareness by taking stock of the progress and satisfaction of his or her work. Every new experience and responsibility holds out opportunities for individuals to understand new facets of themselves and their capacities, a task which is never complete. In most programs of leadership development, self-awareness is the most important element, since it continually funds the process of improvement.

Each college or university will develop its own set of protocols for the annual evaluation, and there will be appropriate variations about what should be written and what may be covered through conversations. Whatever else, the process should feature a written review of the goals that were set the prior year and/or of the expectations that were defined at the time of the president's initial appointment. At the end of the president's first year, of course, the process of review may be more prospective than retrospective, with the issues defined at appointment providing the most important benchmarks.

TOPICS AND CRITERIA IN SELF-ASSESSMENT

TOPICS. What topics and goals are in order for the evaluation? In *Presidential Assessment*, John W. Nason grouped criteria for performance in six categories based on the study of a large number of evaluation processes: (1) academic management and leadership, (2) administrative management and leadership, (3) budget and finance, (4) fundraising, (5) external relations, and (6) personal characteristics. This list offers a quick and useful reference point for presidents composing a self-assessment statement. The list of management and leadership competencies provided in the next chapter concerning comprehensive assessment, as well as the questionnaires in Appendix II, offer illustrations of questions that presidents and boards can also use to focus on key goals and issues in self-assessment. They address several dimensions of leadership and will be helpful to presidents in sorting out the different aspects of their responsibilities.

The board assessment committee should be given the opportunity to review and respond to the topics that the president proposes for the self-assessment. Board members may have questions or issues that they believe should be addressed in the review, so there should be a way for these suggestions to be communicated to the president. This can be accomplished by the president sharing a brief outline of proposed topics with the chair of the board and other members of the committee at the outset of the process. It should be expected that the form and content of the items will vary from year to year, both to avoid repetition and to respond to changing circumstances. The following provides a comprehensive set of possibilities to assist in developing a self-assessment.

> **Some of the most telling goals to be analyzed, reviewed and proposed are those that have been developed through a strategy process that tells the organization's story and defines its vision for the future.**

STRATEGIC PRIORITIES. Some of the most telling goals to be analyzed, reviewed and proposed are those that have been developed through a strategy process that tells the organization's story and defines its vision for the future. Developing and implementing a vision are quintessential elements of leadership. Most strategic plans include a series of basic strategic initiatives and imperatives that set the institution's priorities for the next several years. These should provide the basic framework for the president's self-assessment from year to year. The major strategies will focus on everything from finances to curriculum to enrollment and many things in between. As critical and comprehensive points of leverage, the initiatives reflect the institution's comparative strategic position, its core competencies, its competitive advantages, its vulnerabilities and its aspirations for the future. The strategic directions should embody a series of goals and actions, many of which will be quantifiable or measureable in some form. They will both reflect and incorporate a set of key strategic indicators and performance metrics by which the institution measures its comparative position and progress over time in achieving its vision.

Measureable Goals. Some presidents are hesitant to offer quantitative goals in a strategic plan because of the political and performance risks that they may involve. Unfortunately, they also lose the sharp focus and intense motivation that measurable goals can provide. If, of course, the strategy is still a work in progress early in a presidency, then the president's strategic priorities will be more hypothetical or tentative, though most new presidents already have a good sense of major strategic issues and possibilities.

Annual Priorities and Goals. Since many strategic plans have a plethora of goals and objectives, the president will want to focus each year on those five to 10 priorities and goals that have substantial strategic importance for the immediate future and that require the president's direct involvement. A president may offer comparative, trend and ratio analyses of the metrics concerning these key goals, and highlight the ways that they can be related directly to personal effort and achievement, all of which is especially useful to the governing board. The self-analysis then serves to strengthen communication with the board, provide it with new information, and educate it about future challenges. The goals take on special meaning when they are interpreted in a strategic context as elements required for the fulfillment of the organization's vision. The board should look to the president for precisely this kind of strategic interpretation of the annual goals.

Critical Processes. One of the attractions of the annual review is that it can be used flexibly to address a variety of issues that do not fall neatly into operational or strategic goals. Not every broader topic will be considered every year, and some of them may await the more comprehensive review that is done periodically. Presidents might occasionally use the opportunity to examine and propose ways to address critical processes of management and decision-making that are in need of repair or renewal, and to invite the board's ideas about the wisdom of addressing them. Often presidents find themselves dealing repeatedly with vexing problems that arise from complex or even dysfunctional processes of decision-making that no one has quite the time, energy or courage to address. Some appointment and tenure processes fall into this category, as do planning and budgeting methods, especially during periods of retrenchment. These kinds of questions may ultimately engage the board directly so they can be raised appropriately in an annual evaluation.

KEY RELATIONSHIPS. Other critical areas of university life may also be considered in the annual evaluation, such as issues related to leadership development, organizational and staffing changes, relationships with faculty and students, and succession planning, especially for key members of the president's leadership team. This is a critical leadership area in which the president may wish to develop goals to share with the board since the president's own effectiveness depends so directly on the group's cooperativeness and competence. The effectiveness of relationships with other key constituencies such as alumni and legislators and government officials may also rise to the surface as a priority. It can be appropriate for the president to share goals for making contacts and organizing and attending events both on and off campus.

> The review process should encourage presidents to think deeply about their own satisfaction with the position, and what they have learned about the strengths and weaknesses they bring to their responsibilities.

PERSONAL FULFILLMENT. The review process should encourage presidents to think deeply about their own satisfaction with the position, and what they have learned about the strengths and weaknesses they bring to their responsibilities. The president should have ideas about opportunities for personal and professional development that the board should welcome and consider. Much of the president's effectiveness depends on a large number of competencies and skills, some of which the president may want to strengthen. These questions may be analyzed more fully during a comprehensive review, but considering them annually is part of the same continuous process of leadership development. Included in *Appendix II, Section B* is a series of telling questions that the board of one private college asked its president to answer. They include: "What aspects of your presidency are the most interesting and rewarding to you? Why? What aspects are the least interesting or most difficult for you? Why? What are your short-term personal development objectives and what plans do you have to accomplish them?"[25]

> **Needless to say, many of these issues will not be part of a formal or written presentation, but they can be meaningfully and sensitively considered by a board committee in a private session or with the chair of the board.**

PERSONAL ISSUES. Related questions can also be raised in this context, such as changing family issues, or health considerations that the president might wish to share. Needless to say, many of these issues will not be part of a formal or written presentation, but they can be meaningfully and sensitively considered by a board committee in a private session or with the chair of the board.

LENGTH. The president's written self-evaluation need not be more than five to 10 single-spaced pages, though it is up to each board and president to find a format and a length that is useful to them. Much of the assessment can be presented in bullet points to convey goals and actions, though the more self-reflective sections will clearly need to be in narrative form. In some difficult or special situations, the memorandum might be much longer. The assessment will often include quotations, references and attachments from other reports and from documents that contain a list of goals and metrics, such as a strategic plan, other reports to the board, sections from some accreditation reviews, and the most recently published annual report.

THE BOARD'S REVIEW OF THE SELF-ASSESSMENT

When the committee receives the president's written self-assessment, it will ordinarily circulate it confidentially to other members of the board to invite their responses and suggestions. One question that always arises concerns the form that board responses should take. Since the board's responsibility for the president's appointment and evaluation is so fundamental, it is important to encourage board engagement in the process. If the timing is right, this could be done orally at a meeting, or by each committee member discussing the report with several trustees. It can also be done in writing if the respondents are circumspect about their responses and are confident that they will remain confidential.

> **For the most part, as we have seen, quantitative rating systems and numerical rankings are not useful in the evaluation of a chief executive in higher education.**

In many cases, the chair of the committee should consider soliciting more systematic written responses from board members. Board members who are used to the personnel evaluation and rating forms used in many organizations are sometimes prone to consider using something similar in presidential evaluation. For the most part, as we have seen, quantitative rating systems and numerical rankings are not useful in the evaluation of a chief executive in higher education. The position is singular in the organization, the work is extremely complex and often controversial, authority for decisions is usually shared, and the responsibilities involve relationships with multiple constituencies that are not visible to any single observer.

A simple, open-ended survey form with the basic categories of presidential responsibility as suggested above may be helpful to board members as a way to organize and write their own thoughts, even if they are then provided orally at a meeting. It may also be useful to board members who are not on the assessment committee when they are asked to respond to the president's self-assessment. In some institutions, assessment committees also use an open-ended survey form with the president's knowledge to gain confidential responses from those who work closely and continuously with the president, such as vice presidents and deans. If the opinions are gathered to fill out a perspective that will help the president to be more effective, and the questions are posed in that vein, then there should be no objections to brief and confidential written responses.

> **The delicacy and complexity of a board leader interviewing the president's subordinates has to be carefully considered in the context of each situation, and the risks and benefits that it offers.**

At some colleges and universities the chair of the board or assessment committee leads a small round of direct conversations or interviews with the president's direct reports or leadership team and one or more faculty leaders. The delicacy and complexity of a board leader interviewing the president's subordinates has to be carefully considered in the context of each situation, and the risks and benefits that it offers. The board chair or other leader may be perceived as having conflicts of interest in the outcome of the process, and there will be concerns about an individual's comments getting back to the president. So, the prospect of board-led interviews comes with challenges and issues to confront. In spite of these, some organizational cultures and circumstances, and the credibility and skills of board leaders make the approach possible. If interviews are to occur, they should be with the president's knowledge and counsel, and should follow clear ground rules about confidentiality. The protocols for the interviews should also be defined and shared in advance. In an annual assessment, they should be very limited in scope, and may not be necessary every year. They should also reflect the basic aim of assessment to improve the performance of the president, the leadership team, the board and the institution. (The several sets of questions in *Appendix II* offer many examples of questions that might be used in annual assessment interviews. *Appendix II, Section A* offers an illustration of a basic presidential evaluation form for written responses in an annual assessment.)

FEEDBACK TO THE PRESIDENT

The board committee will want a chance to review and discuss the president's self-assessment, and to consider responses from fellow board members and others in a meeting by themselves. Having done so, they should then discuss their responses with the president in a private meeting. The committee will be able to pose any questions that have occurred to them and their colleagues during their deliberations and seek clarifications and comments on various points from the president. If the committee needs to do so, it can hold a final executive session to draw any conclusions that have arisen from the interaction with the president. At the point that the interactions are complete, the chair of the board, and/or the assessment committee will share their conclusions with the president. In doing so, the chair should convey to the president a clear interpretation of what they have learned during the process, significant aspects of the president's strengths and achievements, and any issues, opportunities and problems that need to be addressed. The chair of the board will then share with the full board the general results of the committee's and the president's conversations. The board's ultimate goal is to contribute to the development of the president's leadership effectiveness, and it should frame its deliberations and comments in these terms.

After the report to the full board, the chair of the board should send a letter or memorandum to the president that describes the process and the general results of the review. This is good policy, and it also serves to document the evaluation for accreditation and other forms of compliance.

MAKING THE MOST OF ANNUAL ASSESSMENT

Having a good process is essential, but it does not guarantee worthwhile results. Both the president and the board have to devote time and energy to make annual assessment a rewarding and worthwhile experience. The president has to develop good information for the board, which in turn has to be conscientious in studying it and reflecting on its own direct involvement with the president. The board needs to be confident that the information that it receives presents a full picture, and that the president's self-analysis is consistent with other information that it has. Some presidents will be self-congratulatory and relate every good thing to their efforts, while others will be unduly modest or hard on themselves. The board has to sort out these tendencies and attend to them if they become barriers to a good process.

In turn, some presidents find that the board focuses on trivial issues, or sends confusing signals based on the different interests and passions of members. Those board members who care most about one specific school or program sometimes orient their evaluations in terms of their priorities and the president's efforts in other areas go unrecognized. Most trustees are able to filter the opinions they hear about the president through the grapevine, but sometimes they fail to do so, especially if a close and trusted friend has had a conflict with the president. For the system to work well, it requires the use of the best available information that is then carefully, conscientiously and judiciously considered.

Given these challenges and cautions, what is the optimum result of an annual assessment? Since leadership development is the primary goal of assessment, it is important for the board to draw out the strengths and the best possibilities of the president in achieving both short and long-term goals. The numbers and narratives in the president's self-assessment that reflect achievement or frustration are essential touchstones in a continuing conversation between the board and the president. They trace the evolution of the presidency and the institution, and they carry weight in building a momentum of success and in profiling problems that require attention.

> **Since leadership development is the primary goal of assessment, it is important for the board to draw out the strengths and the best possibilities of the president in achieving both short and long-term goals.**

More than praise or blame, however, a president hopes to receive clear recognition that the board understands and affirms the value of the strategic agenda that he or she is pursuing. A president's effectiveness is often a function of wise choices about where his or her energy and commitment are invested, and the board's support is critical in confirming those decisions and that investment of leadership capital. An annual assessment should be the time to sharpen the continuing conversation about what matters most to the president and to affirm that his or her vision is both understood and shared by the board, or whether it needs a course correction. If the president has ideas and recommendations about ways to move the agenda forward by re-centering or re-organizing his or her work, pursuing opportunities for personal and professional development, or building on strengths or compensating for weaknesses, it is vital for the board to listen attentively and supportively to those possibilities as well as to offer its own ideas. Additional ideas about leadership development are found in a subsequent chapter on comprehensive assessment.

It also may be possible that warning signals have been sounded through the evaluation that will require the attention of both the board and the president in the coming year. Ways and times to address these problems should be established. The president may benefit from working with a coach or mentor to address problems or issues that have made the board uncomfortable. Some concerns may prompt the board to consider scheduling a more thorough comprehensive assessment and to begin planning to do so with the president's involvement. If the review has produced systematically negative results or reflects an unanticipated loss of confidence by the board and others, then the board should begin considering whether a dignified transition for the president is warranted. Quite frequently, problems arise because a bad match has been made between two otherwise worthy and effective partners, and much grief can be saved if the awareness emerges early in the relationship. These conclusions and decisions should, of course, never be reached or taken lightly, and would require a series of careful discussions among the board committee, the chair, legal counsel, other members of the board and the president. The problems prompting a possible resignation or termination would often reflect issues other than just those related to a single year's performance. They could involve questions that have surfaced about integrity, lack of interest or competence, disagreement about priorities, personal relationships or conflicts of interest. Whatever its nature, the problem would usually require more information and evidence than the annual evaluation itself may have produced.

> **Annual reviews should be scheduled to occur at roughly the same time each year as part of the board's annual schedule of meetings and responsibilities.**

Annual reviews should be scheduled to occur at roughly the same time each year as part of the board's annual schedule of meetings and responsibilities. The worst time to initiate an evaluation process is after a major controversy about the president has arisen, for then board members will be deliberating under intense pressure and possible press coverage, and all sources of information will be colored by emotion and political agendas.

The time for completing an annual evaluation should be not more than one month. If time drags, the goals and issues in the self-assessment will become stale and the process will lose its sense of importance and urgency. Boards are not always consistent and punctual in completing the annual review, and especially in communicating back to the president after their deliberations. The opportunity to create a continuous conversation about the strategic position of the institution and the work of the president gets lost, and the process becomes more of a nagging obligation than an opportunity to improve performance continuously.

Compensation

The annual decision on presidential compensation often unduly controls and drives the annual evaluation process. The reasons are not hard to understand, and the linkage between assessment and compensation is real, but ideally the two processes should be distinct though not unrelated. Those schooled in the corporate world tend to identify "pay" with "financial performance," since the performance generates the resources necessary for the pay, which takes the form of salary, cash bonuses and long-term awards of stock and/or stock options. But the ground rules in academe are different. In the academic world, compensation is essentially salary or deferred compensation, and depends on a series of other factors that relate to the fulfillment of mission, the availability of resources, the compensation of peers, salary history, salary equity, and patterns and competitiveness of compensation for the faculty and staff. Issues related to performance and the development of presidential leadership should be considered on their own terms, and then as one key factor in determining compensation along with the other elements cited above. Although related, they are two separate topics, and the discussions and decisions about them should occur at two different times in different meetings, or following two separate agendas in the same meeting.

Two good AGB resources on compensation policies and practices are *Presidential Compensation in Higher Education: Policies and Best Practices*, by Robert H. Atwell and Jane V. Wellman, and *The Compensation Committee*, a Board Basics booklet by Robert E. Tranquada, M.D.

Checklist for Successful Annual Reviews

The following comments and the checklist are quoted directly, with minor editing, from *Annual Presidential Performance Reviews* by Merrill Schwartz.[26] The list provides a review of good practices for conducting an annual assessment and includes tips on what to avoid. It serves as a useful conclusion to this chapter.

WHAT TO DO

- Lay the foundation for assessment during the search process with clear expectations for performance.
- Establish a board policy for the review process. Consult with the president and revise it as appropriate.
- Base the assessment on agreed-upon strategic goals and benchmarks.
- Make the president's written self-assessment statement the central element in the process.
- Seek legal counsel on confidentiality and open-meeting/open-record laws to clarify what should or will be confidential, especially if yours is a public college or university.
- Complete the process in as short a time as possible (about one month).
- Schedule a private meeting with the president and board committee (including the board chair) to discuss the review. Include a synthesis of the board's feedback on performance.

- Use the review process to agree on goals for the coming year.
- Follow up with appropriate recommendations about compensation adjustments.
- Review the assessment process each year and make needed changes.
- Make annual assessments part of a cycle that includes periodic board self-assessments and comprehensive assessment of the president, or comprehensive joint assessment of the president and board.
- Remember that assessment is not a substitute for regular, ongoing communication between the president, the board, and its leaders.

WHAT TO AVOID

- Don't initiate a review in response to a crisis or event.
- Don't impose a process on the president without providing him/ her with the opportunity to participate in shaping it.
- Don't use rating scales or checklists to collect information about the president—they are ineffective tools that do not fit the process and the presidency.
- Don't delegate the board's responsibility for reviewing the president to other constituents.
- Don't breach confidentiality.
- Don't make the review a meaningless, pro forma exercise.

Case-Study:

From Annual to Comprehensive Assessment at Flagship University[27]

This case study and the one at the end of the next chapter are intended to invite the reader to consider how they would apply the ideas and principles of assessment in concrete terms.

Flagship University annually evaluates its president. The evaluation includes a private discussion between the president and the board's assessment committee regarding the president's written review of annual goals and accomplishments for the previous year, as well as a review of the goals for the coming year. The assessment committee also informally canvases board members to ascertain their views of the president's performance. Since the next year will be the president's fifth, the board wants to do a more formal and inclusive review. While they have been quite pleased with results to date, they are beginning to get rumblings that some find her to be arrogant and unapproachable, particularly when opposing views are expressed. There has been some hint of vindictiveness. The board assessment committee is meeting to decide the kind of assessment to conduct. It needs to determine the sorts of questions to be asked and in what form, who will do the assessment, the groups and individuals to be involved, and other procedural matters. The board chair asks you as a board member for your advice on these matters. What would you propose? How would you respond were you the president?

Chapter IV

Comprehensive Assessment

Comprehensive presidential assessment draws perspectives on the president's effectiveness from interviews with a cross-section of the campus community on a periodic basis. The process is initiated and directed by the governing board with the involvement of the president. It gathers feedback from a variety of sources, including members of the board, faculty, administration, student body, the alumni, the local community and, as appropriate, public officials or church leaders in denominational colleges. The assessment provides the board with information, judgments and opinions about the president's effectiveness based on responses to a systematic set of questions that are asked in the interviews. Most importantly, the process is intended to give the president and the board feedback about ways to strengthen the leadership and work of the president and the institution.

Multi-Level and Multi-Source Evaluation

Since much of the literature on presidential evaluation is legitimately cautious about including any sources of evaluation other than the board, it is important to consider the best ways to gain judgments from individuals and groups with different levels of responsibility in the organization. The strong preference stated in the materials developed by AGB is for interviews of individuals and small groups, and similar ideas are often found concerning the practices of CEO evaluation and leadership development in the corporate world.

USE OF A CONSULTANT

To protect confidentiality and to encourage open expression in the interviews, the AGB literature beginning with John Nason's study consistently recommends the use of an outside consultant. The person should have substantial experience in a presidency or high level academic leadership, though this is not mandatory. Some boards may prefer to employ a consultant with higher education experience from a firm that focuses on leadership assessment and development. In some contexts, one or more trustees or former trustees may have the skills, temperament and objectivity to conduct interviews effectively on the president's performance. This comes with several of the challenges that are noted below, some of which have been reviewed in considering the use of interviews with the president's leadership team during annual assessments.

> In some contexts, one or more trustees or former trustees may have the skills, temperament and objectivity to conduct interviews effectively on the president's performance.

The interviewer or consultant should be someone who inspires the trust of the president, the campus and the board, and who fully understands the academic world. The more the person can draw on knowledge of trends and realities in the leadership of colleges and universities, the more likely the person will be to sort out comments, add perspective and offer useful insights and recommendations. There are financial costs to consider in using a consultant, but also the benefits of saving the board considerable worry, time and energy. The circumstances and characteristics of each board and institution will determine the best approach.

Some cautions are obvious in using anyone connected to the organization, including current or former board members, to lead a comprehensive review that will require multiple time-consuming interviews with a cross-section of the campus and other constituencies. Often board members would be seen as having conflicts or vested interests. Whether justified or not, many faculty and staff members will fear that their views will be discounted in favor of the board's biases, that critical comments will get back to the president, or that the source of comments will become known to other board members, even if this happens unintentionally. These fears will take hold especially if the president is controversial or the institution is facing tough and unpopular financial decisions. Under these circumstances, the board's involvement in the interviews will be seen as suspect since it is also the body that makes final decisions about the president. We can all think of trustees and others who could carry out this tough assignment effectively and transcend criticism from every quarter, such as a distinguished jurist, but the list is not long. Much of the narrative of this study will describe a consultant-oriented process, even though some institutions may choose to do a periodic review in other ways.

INFORMATION FROM CAMPUS INTERVIEWS

The question remains as to how an interview process can use multiple sources to contribute valuable insights and useful information to the board and the president. Whatever information and judgments are gathered, it should be emphasized that it ultimately remains the governing board's responsibility to evaluate and enhance the work of the president.

The fear of undermining the president's authority by seeking opinions about performance from subordinates, faculty and others does not appear to be as decisive a concern in today's environment as it was in earlier literature, though it still exists. [28] In a post Sarbanes-Oxley world, many chief executives in every type of organization, including corporations, routinely undergo periodic evaluations by the governing board that draw directly or indirectly on responses from subordinates. To guarantee its effectiveness, presidential evaluation depends on careful practices and procedures, many of which are defined below. The dangers of distortion, personal attacks, and political agendas are real, so they must be prevented by a fair and disciplined process.

The opportunity to provide the governing board with judgments and information that are not otherwise available outweighs the risks of using multiple sources in a comprehensive evaluation. Governing boards normally include many individuals who have distinguished themselves in both their personal and professional lives, and they often display impressive collective wisdom on complex personnel questions. They can serve as a fair source of evaluation and a resilient sounding board in framing and responding to the president's annual self-evaluations; however, as we have suggested, they are not able to observe and judge the work of the president directly in the everyday contexts of leadership and management.

The goals of comprehensive assessment also focus more sharply and systematically on leadership in a collaborative academic context, and on leadership development. As skilled and experienced as they may be, not many board members are academic professionals, nor have they typically served in positions of leadership in academic communities. The culture of academic decision-making is often foreign to them, and at times perplexing. The perspectives of faculty and staff members, especially of those who work constantly with the president, or who have a special vantage point as a stakeholder, can inform, enlarge and test the governing board's own observations and judgments, especially in setting a course for the next phase of a president's work.

Careful interviews of various sources also can help to correct several of the problems and vulnerabilities that some boards occasionally demonstrate, as we have seen in our review of presidential crises. Presidents often form close friendships or have conflicts with some board members, making it difficult for those individuals to be objective in an evaluation. For all these reasons, the periodic use of a number of sources of evaluation makes eminent sense.

> **As in all evaluations, the most valuable insights come from those who work with the president on a close and continuing basis, and who play a major role in determining the president's success.**

As in all evaluations, the most valuable insights come from those who work with the president on a close and continuing basis, and who play a major role in determining the president's success. Although there are cases of blind loyalty and of active hostility from subordinates, most academic and administrative leaders are now comfortable with the developmental assessment of leadership and management. They practice it in their own spheres of responsibility and it is practiced on them. So vice-presidents, deans, and directors are likely to be valuable sources of insight, especially if they trust the process and the person leading the assessment. Although humans are never without some bias or self-interest, a good process can glean balanced perspectives. Much useful information and good counsel is often locked away in various corners of the organization, which the governing board will never glean unless it is released by a sound method.

For those who are less close to the president and not well informed about the work of the office, the interviews become a valuable source of education about the responsibilities of the president and the board. They also can be focused on larger questions of communication, planning and decision-making where faculty and staff members have direct involvement. Learning of problems or of misperceptions can strengthen the work of the president, especially early in a presidency.

The Interview Process

One of the strengths of an interview process is that it can differentiate questions and responses according to context and circumstance. Questionnaires cannot probe the evidence or take note of a lack of information or political agendas. An interviewer can ask for reasons, examples or data that support a statement. If instruments are administered to dozens of people who are not informed about the work of the president, they provide quantitative averages across groups that do not have much meaning. A "faculty" or "staff" or "student" numerical rating of the president, especially on a large campus, might be useful to learn of perceptions, but it would often be meaningless as a guide to improvement. In other cases, a high rating for a characteristic might mean that one strength is being overplayed and is out of balance. What a high rating on a questionnaire records as a strong point may be so dominant that it becomes a weakness. [29]

> **One of the strengths of an interview process is that it can differentiate questions and responses according to context and circumstance.**

As is also widely acknowledged, instruments have little value unless they are part of a larger interpretive and developmental plan and process for increased effectiveness.[30] As useful as 360-degree evaluations (multi-source and multi-level questionnaires) often can be, their value depends on the quality of insight that comes from knowledgeable participants and consistent follow-up activities that may involve a manager, a human resource professional or an executive coach. However it is done, the benefits of using a variety of sources in a comprehensive periodic evaluation depend on preparation, time, and commitment as well as effective plans for professional development.

One of the basic rules of thumb in periodic presidential evaluation, given the vast differences among institutions, is that one size does not fit all circumstances. Each institution will also have different aims for the evaluation itself in terms of its own evaluation policies and the timing of the review with regard to contract renewal, compensation, strategic initiatives, capital campaigns, and campus controversies.

Governing boards of university systems will ordinarily delegate much of the work of evaluation of individual campus heads to the chief executive of the system, with each campus involving representatives in the process in different ways, guided by system-wide policies. *Appendix II, Section F* includes a detailed set of policies and procedures that guides the annual and comprehensive evaluation of presidents on the campuses of the State University of New York (SUNY) under the overall direction of the chancellor of the system. In the periodic comprehensive process, the head of each campus is evaluated through a multi-source and multi-level process that includes participation by a current or former president from another institution similar to a SUNY campus.

> **While the diversity of institutions is a given, almost all the examples of evaluative criteria and questions rotate around a series of fundamental responsibilities in the work of presidents.**

While the diversity of institutions is a given, almost all the examples of evaluative criteria and questions rotate around a series of fundamental responsibilities in the work of presidents. As we have seen, John Nason found in the 1980s that several basic areas of performance were almost always included in questionnaires addressing the work of presidents. Roughly these same areas are found in the questions proposed by Ingram and Weary as the basis for campus interviews in joint presidential and board reviews. They propose the use of open-ended questions that draw out constructive comments and critiques in a conversational context. (See a list of their proposed interview questions concerning presidential performance in *Appendix II, Section C.*)

INTERVIEW METHODS AND QUESTIONS

The set of interview questions proposed here reflects many of the same dimensions of performance as these earlier accounts, but it provides more internal structure in each topic or theme, focuses more sharply on elements of leadership and translates more directly into opportunities for leadership development. These questions are intended to fulfill the basic purposes of presidential evaluation presented in Chapter II, and they reflect the concept of integral leadership. They are not offered as a rigid oral questionnaire, but should be adapted in each campus circumstance to help initiate and give focus to an interview that has a conversational form. More than anything else, the questions are intended to provide a full illustration of one possibility for guiding the interviews.

LEADERSHIP CONTEXTS AND QUESTIONS

Strategic Leadership

How effectively does the president:

- Demonstrate an understanding of the culture of the organization and convincingly tell its story?
- Use a credible and collaborative strategy process to renew the mission and create a compelling vision?
- Enact the strategy and make things happen to create competitive advantage in responding to and anticipating the driving forces of change and competition?

Educational Leadership

How effectively does the president:

- Assure academic quality by mobilizing resources and using evaluation, evidence, metrics and benchmarking to improve performance continuously in teaching, student learning, research and service?
- Encourage and enable educational and curricular change and innovation?
- Understand and participate in shared academic governance and collaborative decision-making?

Organizational Management

How effectively does the president:

- Manage—analyze, organize, plan, direct, evaluate, improve, renew basic institutional processes and resources (finances, technology, human resources, facilities, services, etc.)?
- Create a sense of urgency, hold others accountable and drive results in key performance areas such as admissions, retention, enrollment, student learning, fund raising, research, service, finances and facilities?
- Make clear, timely and tough decisions?
- Build a talented leadership team and empower and motivate the members to achieve beyond their expectations?

Financial Management

How effectively does the president:

- Understand and manage the organization's financial dynamics, metrics and processes (budgeting, costs, revenues, overhead, balances, and investments) and communicate financial realities to stakeholders?
- Manage resources efficiently and build long-term financial equilibrium (create operating balances, add revenues at a faster rate than expenses, provide for depreciation, and increase the purchasing power of the endowment)?

Fund Raising

How effectively does the president:

- Nurture relationships and obtain gifts and grants at full potential from individuals, alumni, parents, corporations and foundations?
- Engage the board in fund raising?

External Relations

How effectively does the president:

- Establish credibility and influence with external constituencies, such as alumni, public officials, local leaders, parents, and educational associations?
- Gain influence and credibility with the media and increase the visibility and reputation of the institution?

Internal Relations

How effectively does the president:

- Develop a climate and programs that enhance diversity?
- Demonstrate interpersonal skills and sensitivities in relating to individual faculty and staff members and students and show a commitment to their welfare and development?

Board and Governance Relations

How effectively does the president:

- Build a relationship of mutual trust, confidence and open communication with the governing board?
- Develop a good working understanding of the board's, the faculty's and the administration's respective roles in decision-making?

- Focus the board on mission and vision, strategic thinking, resource use and acquisition, and on governance issues that need attention?

Personal Characteristics and Values

How fully and effectively does the president:

- Demonstrate persistence in reaching goals?
- Communicate clearly and convincingly in various forms and contexts?
- Listen?
- Show respect for others?
- Examine and challenge his or her assumptions and show a willingness to explore other viewpoints?
- Build consensus and reconcile conflict between self and others, and among groups and individuals?
- Demonstrate honesty and integrity?
- Inspire trust and confidence?

Summary Questions

- What have been the president's major accomplishments in the leadership of the institution during the past several years?
- What single thing would you suggest to improve the president's effectiveness?
- What other points need to be covered?

Many approaches to interviews are possible. A successful interview can start and end at quite different topics and places, and use a wide variety of methods and questions. It is quite possible, for instance, that a skilled and experienced consultant on leadership in higher education could lead successful interviews by asking highly knowledgeable participants just a few open-ended questions about the president's strengths and weaknesses around terms like trust, inspiration, management, communication, vision, resources and collegiality. With little doubt, though, the interviews eventually would work through most of the features of leadership that the questions above make explicit. Nor would a tacit and streamlined approach be as effective in developing systematic policies concerning evaluation and its purposes, in providing the campus with an understanding of the process, in drawing out perspectives from those who are not especially close to the president's work, and in building an agenda for leadership development. The test for each approach is its ability to gain valid reflections, responses and information from knowledgeable participants on the profile of presidential leadership that the institution intends to use as its point of reference.

The 32 questions provided here represent a full illustration of the type and number of questions and topics that a one-hour interview can be expected to cover. In actual practice, each institution will want to choose questions that reflect the leadership competencies that it finds most illuminating and that best describe its situation and its goals. *Appendix II, Section E* offers examples of questions drawn from other sources, as well as an expanded version of the list provided in the text. One of the early tasks in the assessment process is to ask the president, consultant and board chair (or assessment committee chair) to review the lists and develop an approach and a set of questions for local use.

> The test for each approach is its ability to gain valid reflections, responses and information from knowledgeable participants on the profile of presidential leadership that the institution intends to use as its point of reference.

There are various ways to use the questions to draw out brief but pertinent responses from those being interviewed. The interviewer may choose to read several questions at a time to characterize an area of performance and to elicit responses. As noted below, even though they will have seen them in advance, many respondents are not familiar with the full scope and details of the president's work and may need several prompts to form a response. Interviewees would not be asked questions for which they have no relevant experience, so questions will vary depending on the responsibilities and backgrounds of those being interviewed. In many cases, interviewers can choose key words and phrases from the questions and not read the whole text. Many of those interviewed will have prepared carefully for the session, so a single word or phrase will trigger a response. Concerning the questions on personal characteristics, for example, the interviewer might say, "Since you've examined the specific questions, which of the terms and phrases seems to describe best the president's characteristics and relationships, and which do not?" If there is a lack of clarity in the answers, the interviewer can return to the full questions and ask for examples.

The questioner should not "lead" the respondent to any conclusions by stating a premise or a tentative finding in a question. After several interviews suggesting the president is aloof, for example, an interviewer might be tempted to ask, "Is the president really as aloof as people say?" which unfairly loads the question. The questions also should be "economic" in minimizing ambiguities and variables, though they can be more complex than if they were to be quantified.

Leadership Effectiveness

The emphasis in the questions is on the basic criterion of leadership effectiveness, which places the focus on achievements, organizational relationships, responsibilities, behaviors, practices and goals rather than on the fixed aspects of personality. This central point of reference presupposes that there are many forms and patterns of effective leadership. The term also keeps the conversation realistic, since effectiveness means achieving intended and expected goals. The criteria do not define a heroic or transformational expectation for leadership, although the questions will reveal that exceptional leadership may take these forms. The questions use basic or active verb forms like "manage," "build," "create," "demonstrate," "communicate," and so forth, to fill out the various facets of effectiveness. It is quite clear what effectiveness involves in the context and content of each question. Modifiers and additional criteria for effectiveness are used in some questions when they are needed to highlight important aspects of leadership.

ELEMENTS OF LEADERSHIP

The questions also reflect a variety of dimensions of presidential leadership including the legitimate and effective use of authority, competencies in managerial decision-making, abilities in critical organizational practices like strategy, expertise in educational leadership, and personal attributes, characteristics and values that inspire confidence and trust. The respondents are asked to interpret these characteristics based on their knowledge, observations, opinions, and experiences. Although the interviewees' perspectives will reflect complex and subjective interpretations, the interviewer should seek reasons and warrants for the claims that are made. Since most of the questions focus on observable behavior, decisions and accomplishments, many of them can be measured and supported by information.

> The questions are intended to provide a window into some of the inner dynamics of integral and integrative leadership in collegial settings.

The questions are intended to provide a window into some of the inner dynamics of integral and integrative leadership in collegial settings. Leadership involves many things in different times and contexts, but it always means influencing and mobilizing others to adopt and enact shared purposes, typically in dealing with various forms of change and conflict. The questions reflect the current literature on the theory and practice of leadership as an interactive process, as suggested in AGB's concept of integral leadership and in other studies of presidential leadership in higher education.

ELEMENTS OF LEADERSHIP DEVELOPMENT

The questions and the responses to them also provide the foundation for an emphasis on leadership development. When they are analyzed and interpreted, it becomes apparent where strengths reside, improvements can be made and opportunities present themselves. The key is to bring the possibilities into the self-awareness of the president, who can then respond with the support of the board. The process should reveal and focus on the ways leadership can be made more effective based on the president's own profile of leadership characteristics. Some characteristics are attributes that relate to the givens of personality, and cannot be altered in basic ways, while others focus more on behavioral tendencies that are open to change over time. People can and do gain novel self-understandings and learn new competencies and skills throughout their lives, so leadership development can target the enlargement of awareness and the improvement of abilities. In a leadership context, the focus of development is on ways to use talents and capacities, and foster organizational practices and relationships as resources to influence others to fulfill a common purpose.

Several examples illustrate these points. The improvement of some competencies may be a matter of improving technical skill and knowledge, such as a fuller understanding of financial metrics, while in other cases it may take more work and time to address behavioral tendencies, like a weakness in listening skills, or a tendency to manipulate and manage information. Often the tasks for improvement will involve others in the organization, as the president tries to implement a new organizational practice, such as a novel approach to strategy or to annual or long-range budgeting. In other cases, it may be that the president's vision is not fully understood because it has not been effectively and persistently communicated, and its inspirational potential is falling short.

Awareness of personal characteristics that are not easy to change brings other benefits. Even though, for example, strong analytical thinkers may never become skilled in the holistic sensitivities of intuitive thinking, it benefits everyone to understand how they themselves and the different individuals with whom they work see the world through different lenses and act on it with different personalities. Meyers-Briggs type personality profiles typically bring those points home effectively.

> **By their organization and content, it is clear how the interview questions relate to the various dimensions of leadership.**

By their organization and content, it is clear how the interview questions relate to the various dimensions of leadership. The interviewers and the interviewees should be able to treat the topic systematically and creatively in an open-ended exchange without a rigid format of responses. Taken together, the questions transparently address many facets of leadership that can be translated into both an analysis of performance and an agenda for development.

Reference Points: Balance and Integration

Several reference points and summary questions can be used by an interviewer to orient the process, to draw out various interpretive themes and to clarify responses. If the conversation rambles or people seem reluctant to come to conclusions, the interviewer can try to find patterns of agreement or disagreement by asking whether the president meets, exceeds or falls below expectations on the issue under discussion. The responses will then move people to justify their answers by giving more specific information or reasons for their views.

In terms of leadership development possibilities, there are several patterns that become obvious in each set of topics. One is whether the president's leadership shows an active balance among different leadership strengths within a given leadership theme. Some of the questions concerning strategic leadership, for example, focus on "understanding" a culture and "creating" a vision, which are ways of thinking and conceptualizing, while another asks about "enacting" the strategy and "making things happen," which requires various forms of action. One of the key tests of strategic leadership is precisely the ability to translate a conceptual vision into reality. Both sides of the thinking/acting equation have to be satisfied for leadership in organizations to be fully successful. Effective organizational leaders are often "beautiful realists" who demonstrate a reciprocal balance between conceptualizing and institutionalizing a course of action, so the interviewer should be sensitive to similar patterns in each theme.

> **One of the key tests of strategic leadership is precisely the ability to translate a conceptual vision into reality.**

Under the management area, to give another example, there is a question about the president's effectiveness in "driving results" and another about "motivating and empowering others." If leaders push too hard to control things while driving results, they typically fail to delegate responsibilities and empower others, which over time will damage peoples' levels of motivation and initiative. Sensitivity to the relationship among questions helps the interviewer to create an active dialogue in the interview, and to come back to questions with a concern for leadership balance and opportunities for leadership development.

In many cases, interviewers also will be able to see different profiles and patterns of presidential leadership as they emerge *across* the different topics. The topics and questions explore different frames of thinking and problem-solving in which presidents must be competent. Looking across the questions, several characteristic ways of making sense of problems and solving them are in focus, including strategic, managerial, collegial, political and relational or interpersonal orientations or styles. [31]

Presidential Leadership Orientations

Political: places an emphasis on using persuasion, influence and authority to satisfy interests, create coalitions, and build consensus, and/or to isolate and sanction opponents.

Managerial: emphasizes the development of effective and efficient financial and administrative decision-making systems and processes, organizational structures and lines of accountability, and coherent policies, rules and regulations.

Collegial: stresses the importance of processes of shared academic governance and collaborative decision-making as basic norms of legitimacy.

Relational: sees the centrality of attracting and developing human talent and relying on interpersonal skills and relationships to create motivation and effectiveness, teamwork and productivity, trust and commitment.

Strategic: emphasizes the centrality of knowing and telling the organization's story and understanding its culture, and developing and implementing an integrative vision to respond to change and prepare for the challenges of the future.

Most leaders tend to favor several of these broad forms of seeing and thinking about issues, and it is helpful to bring them to light, especially for the president's self-awareness. Since the work of a president requires multiple sensitivities and skills to deal effectively with the integrated complexity of real world problems, it is very beneficial for leaders to be able to balance and integrate these different orientations to fit the occasion, choosing and combining the right tools for the job. Especially is this so in the context of integral leadership and the development of a shared strategic vision. The ability to integrate purposes (mission and vision) and processes (managerial, political, relational, strategic and collegial) becomes an overarching test of effective leadership. Over time, leaders can sharpen their skills and sensitivities to areas in which they are less naturally prone, especially as they become aware of their patterns. In some cases the interviewer will hear these themes emerging naturally in the conversations and will be able to highlight perceptions of different leadership orientations as part of a useful interpretive summary.

Disqualification

In most cases, the interviews will confirm the ways presidents have tried to draw on their strengths and to limit their weaknesses. In some few cases, however, the interviews may find some dangerous forms of weakness that are not easily improved by focused effort, but that are corrosive, or even toxic. They can be "derailers" that take the train off the track. They are a special class of weaknesses that systematically undermines the president's leadership effectiveness. Sometimes the incumbents in presidencies are miscast for the role—as talented, honorable and bright as they otherwise may be. At other times, presidents find themselves working under enormous stress that brings out unanticipated changes in their behavior. Many of the leadership questions have an underside that could surface in the interviews, and they represent characteristics that can be the keys to understanding how and why a presidency may be unraveling. If interviewers begin to see patterns forming around perceived presidential behavior in terms of "disqualifiers," such as arrogance, dishonesty, aloofness, perfectionism, manipulativeness, closed-mindedness, rigidity, distrustfulness, volatility, sycophancy or incompetence, then the process may make need to shift gears and take account that it is heading into difficult straits.[32] If these tendencies reach a threshold of concern, they should become the focus of a plan to deal with the problems in an ongoing process of leadership development, as discussed in the next chapter.

A leading executive coach, Marshall Goldsmith, provides clear and concrete examples of how to recognize the disqualifiers that may undercut the effectiveness of otherwise successful and intelligent leaders. In providing a list of bad habits of behavior to watch out for, he notes, among others, such specifics as "winning too much," "passing judgment," "making destructive comments," "starting with 'no,'" "telling the world how smart we are," "speaking when angry," "withholding information," "making excuses," "failing to express gratitude," "failing to give recognition," "playing favorites," "clinging to the past," and "not listening."[33] Each of these instances of behavior can be more than annoyances. If they become persistent or prolonged, they can destroy effective reciprocal leadership. As disqualifiers, they damage the heart of the leadership relationship by showing disrespect for the partners in shared governance. Depending on circumstances and the depth of the problem, the systematic re-orientation or even the termination of a presidential appointment could be at issue rather than its incremental improvement.

Happily, most evaluations will not have to deal with systematic disqualifiers, but bringing milder instances of them to awareness can be a strong and healthy tonic for persons who hold high positions. As we have suggested, the aim of the interview process is to provide feedback to the president and the board on the enhancement of performance, not to create a list of isolated faults and weaknesses, or of praise for a disembodied list of achievements. Approaches that raise a president's awareness of strengths and create a design of ways to balance and integrate them will be far more motivating and will sustain a commitment to leadership development over time.

Case-study:

The Comprehensive Assessment Report at Flagship University

Flagship asked the well-regarded former president of another institution in the state to provide his assistance in leading the comprehensive assessment of the president. He asked for brief written responses about the president's performance from the board and the vice presidents, and then interviewed each of them individually. He also held a series of small group meetings with members of the faculty, staff, student body, and the alumni association as well as with local leaders from the community. In all, he had contact with over 100 individuals. The consultant's report was delivered to the board's assessment committee and revealed a goal-oriented president who had achieved major positive results in five years, especially concerning Flagship's financial position. However, a large number of both internal and external constituents gave alarming examples of her response to people who held views different from hers. The report gave examples of "dressing down people publicly," "isolating dissenters," and, in several cases, shouting in public meetings. Several respondents claimed to know people who were fired for their dissent. Her many defenders, while acknowledging she could be brittle at times, praised her for all that has been accomplished since her arrival. The chair and the assessment committee have to decide what to say to her. What would you say to the president were you on the assessment committee? How would you respond to the assessment were you the president?

Chapter V

Procedures and Protocols in Comprehensive Assessment

Much of the effectiveness of a periodic comprehensive assessment depends on careful preparation and planning as well as a shared understanding of its goals and procedures. Its methods have to embody sensitivity to the purposes it serves and an understanding of both the general and local norms of academic culture. Getting the procedures and protocols right is a critical element in the success of the process.

This overview describes and illustrates an assessment that is led by a board committee that uses an outside consultant and an interview-based protocol. It discusses the role of the president, board, assessment committee, consultant, and participants in the interviews.

Just as with annual assessment, but even more clearly, the institution will need to obtain legal advice about open meeting and open record laws and how they might apply to the comprehensive assessment of the president. A comprehensive assessment has many elements that need to be scrutinized to assure compliance with state law.

Regular Process

The literature agrees in stressing that a periodic comprehensive process should follow a regular schedule and take place every three to four years. The author suggests, in agreement with policies at the State University of New York, that it is wise to have a review after the president's first three years in office in order to address any early problems that might become serious or to affirm the initial progress of a talented leader. Since the review contributes so much to the board's own responsibilities to monitor the institution's evolution, a three- to four-year cycle makes good sense in terms of the board's own work. In many cases it would be useful to have a joint presidential and board assessment three or four years after the president's first comprehensive review. If a board is aware that a president intends to retire or resign in the next year or so, then a comprehensive review would not fit the circumstances.

As explained earlier, a comprehensive assessment should normally not be initiated in response to a crisis in presidential confidence or at the time of a public controversy over an event or decision. Nor should it be seen as a way to gain evidence for a termination decision that a board already intends to make. To do so is to compromise the purposes of the process itself. Assessment should be regularly scheduled around predictable times, circumstances and needs, and the process should be agreed to in advance by the president and the board.

> **To be sure, even regularly scheduled evaluations will occur in a wide variety of circumstances, and the precise timing will have to be tailored to the needs of the institution.**

To be sure, even regularly scheduled evaluations will occur in a wide variety of circumstances, and the precise timing will have to be tailored to the needs of the institution. Clarifying purposes and defining the specific objectives of the review under different circumstances are essential steps. Some boards will plan the assessment to coincide with pending decisions on contract renewal. Although appraisal of performance is not solely for the purpose of contract renewal, it obviously provides information that is essential for the board's decision. At other times, an assessment will be helpful in considering the president's and the institution's readiness for a capital campaign or a major new strategy process.

In some cases, the process will turn up unexpected pockets of hostility or negative appraisals, complicating a review. The political and academic currents of campus decision-making are forever shifting, and controversies can consume a campus with little warning. As a result, chances are high that something will be different about the findings of a review than was anticipated at the outset. Tough issues and circumstances will need to be dealt with nimbly, consistent with the chair's leadership, the board's authority, the president's advice and the purposes of the process. The details of the procedures may need to be modified as conditions and unexpected findings suggest. Interviews may have to be added, for instance, or information from some sources reviewed or verified before the process can be completed.

RESPONSIBILITIES OF THE BOARD, PRESIDENT AND STAFF

An effective assessment depends on the full and clear support of both the chair of the board, other board leaders and the president. As a board plans a comprehensive review, it will ordinarily want to create an assessment committee to sponsor the process. Some boards will have a standing committee that can oversee the evaluation, though the committee should typically not have more than five or six members, all of whom have time to give to the assignment. The chair of the board should ordinarily be an active member of the committee, typically its chair, and the president should be an *ex officio* member who is fully engaged in the process. In some contexts, a faculty or staff member may be a useful participant.

Once the board has decided on the basic outline of the review, it should develop a resolution for board action that will charge the committee with the authority and the resources to complete the review. The resolution can be brief and simple if the board already has adopted a standing policy on presidential evaluation. (See *Appendix I, Section A* for an illustration and set of principles.) On this basis, the board can move forward to set up a timetable for the evaluation, block out time for consideration of the process and the reports at subsequent meetings, and decide whether they wish to seek a consultant.

The governing board should be kept informed of the major steps in the evaluation. The campus at large should also be notified that the board is conducting a review and told of the timeline for the process. The board will need to communicate again with the campus community when the evaluation has been completed.

The chair of the assessment committee will involve the president in planning the evaluation, and they will be the primary contacts with the consultant in authorizing basic arrangements for the interviews. The president or board will also make available a staff member to schedule meetings, distribute information and assist the consultant with other administrative details and local travel and logistical arrangements. The diligence and effectiveness of staff support is one of the essential keys to assuring the preparedness and productiveness of the process. Interviewees need to know and be reminded of the importance of the process, understand their role in it, receive materials on time and prepare for the session in advance.

BACKGROUND INFORMATION

One of the benefits of periodic assessment is that it places the results of annual evaluations into a larger context. Goals that require several years to be achieved can be reviewed within a longer time-frame. To accomplish this, the president should provide the consultant two or three earlier annual self-assessments and board responses in order to give a flavor of prior issues and goals. The consultant should also receive a copy or summary of the institution's current strategic plan, its fact book, summary financial data, minutes of the past several board meetings, board by-laws, admissions, capital campaign and alumni publications, and the most recent accreditation visiting team report and the institution's response to it. Some institutions provide the president with a detailed set of expectations on appointment. This agreement should be provided since it may need to become part of the assessment criteria. The president should also prepare a self-assessment as part of the periodic evaluation. It should highlight the time frame for the review and provide a context for the president's interview with the consultant.

> **The first meeting is critical in establishing mutual confidence and clarifying expectations, and much of the effectiveness of the assessment will flow from the shared understanding that is achieved.**

CAMPUS VISIT: THE SCOPE OF THE TASK

Although circumstances will vary widely, there are several key elements that the board should expect and monitor in the consultant's work with the institution. The first phase involves a visit to the campus to meet the president and the assessment committee chair, the chairman of the board, other committee members, and support staff. The first meeting is critical in establishing mutual confidence and clarifying expectations, and much of the effectiveness of the assessment will flow from the shared understanding that is achieved. There is a benefit in arranging for the consultant to attend some part of a board or committee meeting, both to meet key trustees on the assessment committee in one place and to see how the board and the president conduct their business. During this phase, the consultant, the board's assessment committee and the president discuss the purposes and goals of the process, review the criteria and define the interview questions and methodology, and discuss the number and the format of interviews to be conducted. Timelines should be defined, dates for interviews projected and required notices and materials planned. The meetings should be oriented toward finalizing the scope of the review, including the type of oral and written reports that are anticipated, as discussed below. Whatever details are not finalized during the first visit can be handled by phone and e-mail at an early date after the meeting. If there is time, the initial visit can be an opportune moment to interview the president and perhaps the chair of the board.

> **The interviews should focus on those who are in a position to contribute most to the president's success and who know his or her work best.**

Typically, the board should expect a consultant to come to the campus at least three times: an initial visit with the president and assessment committee, a second visit of several days for interviews, and the final visit to present and discuss the report. The size of the institution and other factors will influence the number of visits and days involved. In many cases, budgets and resources will drive the decisions. Based on study and experience, Nason, Ingram and Weary, and Schwartz all suggest that the total process should not exceed four months to avoid loss of focus and to prevent speculation or rumors about the fate of the president. Boards that meet only three or four times a year may wish to begin and conclude the process to coincide with board meeting dates.

THE INTERVIEWS

The assessment committee should decide which individuals and groups should be interviewed, and assure that no relevant group is denied an opportunity to be heard or otherwise represented. The interviews should focus on those who are in a position to contribute most to the president's success and who know his or her work best. Local culture will determine the proprieties, but the whole process will be weakened if it is perceived to be screened or managed. The interviews will normally take from four to six or more days, depending on the size of the campus and the number of interviewees. In large campuses it may require two consultants to complete the interviews, or extra visits by one consultant. Although they are not ideal, phone interviews can be an efficient way to gather information from key individuals who cannot be interviewed in person.

> **The reality of time and budget may require some compromises on the number of interviews and the size of groups, but the interview method becomes less useful the larger the group.**

The interviews should be guided by questions that have been circulated to the participants in advance and conducted either one-on-one or in small groups. The reality of time and budget may require some compromises on the number of interviews and the size of groups, but the interview method becomes less useful the larger the group. Lengthy individual interviews of at least 90 minutes are recommended for the president, board chair, and assessment committee chair (if not also the board chair). Board members and/or leaders (in large boards), and administrative leaders, such as vice presidents and deans (in smaller institutions), and a designated faculty leader should also have individual meetings, though the interviews can be briefer. The trustees of large boards can be interviewed in small groups, as can various cross-sections of the faculty. Those who interact less with the president, and stakeholders such as alumni or community leaders, can meet in larger groups and will be asked fewer questions since their direct knowledge of all aspects of the president's work is likely to be more limited. As institutions consider whom to include in the interviews, the answers will come readily: officers of the faculty senate or its equivalent, deans and vice presidents, the head of the staff organization, the leaders of various key faculty committees, faculty who have been recognized for their teaching and scholarship, a group of junior faculty, a representative number of chairs of academic departments, a select group of heads and members of administrative departments, student and alumni leaders, and local officials and community leaders. Each campus will have its own natural list.

The staff member who serves the assessment committee will want to assure that the intended representative cross-section of the campus is involved and will work with the chair of the committee and president to that end. If it is anticipated that there are individuals or groups with strong resentments or heavy complaints, they should not all be grouped into the same interview sessions. Even though groups with very mixed opinions ordinarily sort themselves out quite well, and people in the interviews generally listen and respect different points of view, there is no reason to risk a concentration of strong feelings. During each session, the interviewer tries to keep a balance of opportunities for different people to speak, and emphasizes the confidentiality of the process.

> **The value of the process depends on the degree to which people have thought seriously about the issues and are ready to contribute their best thinking in the interviews.**

A memorandum including a description of the process, questions to guide the interviews, and a current profile of information about the institution (such as its dashboard of strategic indicators, a recent annual report by the president, or a summary of the strategic plan) should be provided in advance to those to be interviewed. The participants should be asked explicitly to study the interview questions and to be familiar with the institutional profile. The value of the process depends on the degree to which people have thought seriously about the issues and are ready to contribute their best thinking in the interviews. The sample letter of invitation and the description of the process provided in *Appendix I, Section B* make it clear that participants should provide relevant backing for their opinions and can be assured of the confidentiality of their views.

Written and Oral Reports

The reports that present the findings of the evaluation will take different written and oral forms depending on the needs and circumstances of each institution and the advice of the consultant. Since the options can have several permutations, it is best to start with a quick summary. There will ordinarily be three reports: (1) a written summary of the *process*, (2) an oral and/or written analysis and interpretation of the interviews focused on *performance* and (3) written and oral *recommendations* of ways to address issues and improve effectiveness. The president should be given the opportunity to review and comment on the performance report and the recommendations before they are presented to the board. The consultant should also enlarge on the written recommendations concerning the president's professional development in a separate private meeting with the president.

THE PROCESS REPORT

The Process Report is easy to describe. It is a written report on the approach taken to the interviews, and the names, roles and responsibilities of those who participated. The report will outline the scope and dates of meetings and interviews and when various tasks were completed. It can be shared widely and openly, and it serves to document the assessment for accreditation and other purposes. It will ordinarily be about two to three pages long.

THE PERFORMANCE REPORT

The consultant's basic task is to provide an analysis and interpretation of the feedback from the interviews that will be useful in evaluating and improving the president's leadership. The Performance Report should follow the main lines of the several topics and themes of the interviews, and will highlight areas of perceived stronger or weaker presidential performance, other organizational issues that merit attention, and the intensity that people feel about various questions. As we have noted in our discussion of feedback from the interviews, the consultant will focus on consistencies and disparities in the comments and interpret patterns of response that arise from the data, often using apt phrases and brief quotes that capture common sentiments. The report will have to paraphrase any ugly or *ad hominem* remarks, and should protect the identity of the speaker, but the tone and content of the meetings should be captured. There may be, for instance, clear differences of opinion among faculty from different disciplines, or among administrators depending on their level of responsibility and frequency of contact with the president. Often the apparent reasons for the differences will be noted in the report.

> ...the consultant will focus on consistencies and disparities in the comments and interpret patterns of response that arise from the data, often using apt phrases and brief quotes that capture common sentiments.

Authorities on presidential evaluation have different opinions about whether the Performance Report should be presented orally or in writing to the governing board. The report conveys confidential details of perceptions of the president's leadership, so it necessarily covers sensitive issues. Anything in writing could become public, especially under some state rules, and in some hostile contexts could unfairly damage the president, or inadvertently disclose the confidential views of groups or individuals. If the environment is toxic and the president's interests are harmed, then the consultant's report might become a point of legal contention by an unhappy president, or the report could become an object of public scrutiny and commentary by the president's critics or supporters. For these reasons, providing the Performance Report orally is often advisable, and is worth careful consideration. The decision has to be made in the context of each institution's needs and circumstances, the findings of the report, legal standards, the board and the president's preferences and the consultant's advice.

Institutions will differ on the need and benefits of a written report. Private institutions in particular may have traditions of board governance and decision-making that create an expectation for something in writing, based in part on a demonstrated ability to keep sensitive information confidential. For various reasons, many public institutions will also request to have a written report, even though the report could often become public. Institutions frequently want a deliberate and considered dialogue among board members and the president based on their study of and reflection about the consultant's written report. If the board is unified and the report reflects largely positive findings, a carefully drawn written report will not be problematic. Nor will it stir much interest if it does become public. If the board is divided on controversial issues, then the confidentiality of the report will be at risk and it might contribute to the conflict.

Because of the fluidity and uncertainly of these kinds of circumstances, the consultant should draft the written Performance Report as a confidential document that he or she knows might well become public. Scrupulous care should be taken not to disclose directly or inadvertently the identity of anyone who has offered comments. The consultant should be careful not to commit to writing any thoughtless or hostile personal comments that would damage the president or others, especially when taken out of context. The report should display the balance, circumspection and evidence-based analysis of a professional document. In sensitive areas or where the findings are ambiguous, the report should be written in general terms, and more specific comments provided orally as appropriate. The consultant will need to know as much as possible about the potential fate and use of the report and its status before preparing it, and often will need to clear it with his or her sponsoring organization. As a basic principle, the consultant would never make any public comments about the report, which is fully controlled by the board once it is completed. Performance reports tend to run eight to 10 single-spaced pages, though the length can vary widely if there are special issues or problems. The basic task is to cover adequately the content of the interviews around each of the elements of presidential effectiveness.

RECOMMENDATIONS FOR IMPROVEMENT

Most boards and presidents will also expect the consultant to provide a set of Recommendations for Improvement as part of the assessment. They will ask, "Based on what we have learned, what should we do?" They will want advice on what the assessment adds up to, suggestions and recommendations about ways to address some of the opportunities, problems or conflicts revealed in the interviews, and what general types of plans and actions concerning leadership development the president, the board and the institution should consider.

Most boards will want these broader recommendations in writing, especially if they offer suggestions that are based on trends and "best practices" at other colleges and universities. Since the recommendations can and should be written in the context of seeking improvements, there should not be major worries in their taking written form. Although it would be considered a private and confidential communication to the board, some parts of the report could be summarized in the communication to the campus at the conclusion of the assessment. A set of recommendations would normally be four to five single-spaced pages, though it will find its own length to deal with topics that arise in the interviews. The report will often include references to books, articles, policy statements and programs that the board and president may wish to consult and to consider.

The consultant's suggestions should be based on findings from the interviews, documents that were provided by the institution, and knowledge of developments in higher education, and should never be an independent expert's personal appraisal of the effectiveness of the president, or a judgment about contract renewal. These considerations are reserved strictly for the governing board.

Institutions will usually request that the consultant present or discuss the report at a board meeting, or with the board chair and assessment committee, who will in turn present it to the board. The chair will decide, with the advice of the president and the consultant, whether the president should attend the session where the consultant presents the report. As suggested earlier, the president should always have a chance to hear or read the reports and review them for factual accuracy and for comment before they are presented to anyone else. The consultant should also provide the president with an opportunity to delve more deeply into the possibilities for professional development in a private conversation. A president has very few opportunities to have a disinterested conversation with a knowledgeable peer about his or her professional future and ideas to improve performance. The conversation could be a useful trigger for the president to develop plans to address issues that have surfaced through the assessment.

The chair of the board has a significant role to play in assuring that the findings of the reports are translated into appropriate forms of action and follow-up steps and do not get lost in the press of daily business. Although there is no script to define a board chair's responsibilities since they vary so widely by institution and circumstance, there are several guiding norms for boards to follow. Whatever else, the chair should assure that the findings are used appropriately in separate but related deliberations on compensation and contract renewal, that the results of the comprehensive review are translated into subsequent annual reviews, and that a strong link is forged between appraisal and leadership development. Some of the results may target quite specific goals and metrics that the president and others will be expected to address and that will be reviewed continually. Others will take the form of suggestions to improve leadership competencies and will depend primarily on the president's initiative and responsibility. It may also be the case that some of the priorities defined in the reports point to governance issues that make a claim on the board's own agenda for consideration and action.

> **...it is not the responsibility of the chair to be an expert on collegial leadership. To do so would be to confuse roles and to draw the chair too deeply into the president's own personal responsibility for professional improvement.**

None of this means that the chair of the board has to assume the role of a manager or executive coach in taking responsibility for designing and providing growth opportunities for the president. The chair should encourage and support the development of possibilities that the president finds worthwhile, approve funding as needed, and assure that the activities are taking place and that they are meeting the president's expectations. In some cases the chair's professional experience and his or her relationship with the president may make it appropriate for the chair to offer counsel from time to time at the president's request on improving leadership competencies or resolving conflicts. This may especially be so concerning issues with a bearing on governance. However, it is not the responsibility of the chair to be an expert on collegial leadership. To do so would be to confuse roles and to draw the chair too deeply into the president's own personal responsibility for professional improvement.

Leadership Development: Plans and Actions

The assessment will typically offer findings that are useful to the president at a number of levels, from issues of behavior and forms of organizational practice to a new level of self-understanding. Most evaluations will affirm the president's work but will typically cite the need for greater effectiveness in such areas as communication, collegial governance, financial decision-making, fund raising or other central elements of the president's work. Sometimes the feedback represents a misunderstanding of complex policies and procedures, which the president and staff members can then seek to address through various lines of communication or by changes in practices. In other cases the president and the board will be surprised and even bewildered by the ways a presidential comment, action or decision has been interpreted, which may well call for a concerted effort to change the ways the president discusses issues. Some concerns will address broader operational and strategic problems that are not of the president's making, but that can be addressed by the president and the board through a series of initiatives to respond to the ideas and challenges surfaced in the interviews.

> **The board should also take the time to "assess the assessment" and to ask itself what it has learned from the process.**

The board should also take the time to "assess the assessment" and to ask itself what it has learned from the process. Does it remain basically a compliance event in which people go through the motions and then quickly move on to other business? Or has the process been integrated into several of the other central responsibilities of the board that engage its members? When set in the right framework of ideas and processes concerning leadership, comprehensive assessment has the potential to give the board a powerful mechanism to deepen its own responsibilities to monitor, evaluate, and improve the president's effectiveness and the quality of the organization. The board shifts from being an observer of the president's leadership to becoming an active partner with the president and others in integral leadership.

SELF-AWARENESS AND LEADERSHIP DEVELOPMENT

The evaluation will be most influential to the extent that it offers awareness and insight at the level of the president's self-understanding. A periodic evaluation gives the president a chance to get distance on the meaning of his or her leadership and the satisfactions and challenges that it brings. Does the president continue to have a passion for the work and the purposes that it serves? Is the university's strategy, for example, more than a list of goals, but the articulation of a vision in which the president is personally invested? The assessment should communicate a sense of how well the community understands and accepts the strategic direction and priorities of the institution and what the president may need to do to renew or explain it. The evaluation should lead the president to ask and to analyze whether time and energy are being directed to issues that matter most, or whether the president has become a prisoner of the office, the schedule and the cycle of daily dramas. How does the president gain more control of the strategic agenda, and find renewal and purpose in doing so?

> **The power and potential of the assessment reside in capturing and interpreting feedback in ways that make it a continuing source of improvement.**

In a similar vein, how does the president use the feedback provided through the process to deepen self-awareness about the competencies, practices, relationships, responsibilities and actions that are dimensions and resources of leadership? The power and potential of the assessment reside in capturing and interpreting feedback in ways that make it a continuing source of improvement. The consultant's report should highlight strengths and define the issues that offer the most opportunity for development, or that may require immediate attention. The evaluation may show that the president is relying too heavily on the political and managerial aspects of leadership and neglecting the collegial, educational and inspirational dimensions of the work. Or, as we have noted, strengths may be overplayed and become weaknesses. If an evaluation shows that the campus leader is perceived in ways we cited as "disqualifiers," then the president's leadership will be subverted over time, whether or not he or she continues to hold office. Any of these warning signs should be addressed in short order and carefully reviewed at the next annual assessment.

PRESIDENT'S DEVELOPMENT PLAN

A periodic assessment should encourage the president to create a set of leadership development goals and plans, many of which should be shared in general terms with the chair of the board and the assessment committee. This might involve engaging the same or another consultant as a coach or mentor in developing the details of a development plan, especially if it relates to skills and abilities in relationships. In many cases, the evaluation will focus on organizational policies or practices that need to be revised or renewed, requiring the leadership of the president and often the involvement of the board. In other cases, it may have become apparent that the board and president need to strengthen their own working relationship and that it is time for the board to conduct an evaluation of its own effectiveness.

A leadership development plan for the president should build on strengths and reinforce achievements. A president's notable capacity for hard work and rigorous conceptual analysis, for example, should be affirmed by the board but may need to be balanced by greater attention to the development of political skills and sensitivities. Talents in key results areas like fund raising or legislative relations should be used to full advantage while assuring that the agenda for educational leadership is being advanced and carefully monitored by the president. Some presidents will have powerful abilities in educational and curricular areas, and their influence and intellect in these domains should be spotlighted and deployed. If they lack a command of financial issues, they will want to increase their knowledge and assure that others have the expertise they lack. In general terms, staff support and leadership may have to complement areas in which the president does not have exemplary skill, even as the president is given the opportunity to enlarge his or her knowledge and competencies.

> **Talents in key results areas like fund raising or legislative relations should be used to full advantage while assuring that the agenda for educational leadership is being advanced and carefully monitored by the president.**

Presidents can often gain more expertise in key decision-making areas like finance, marketing, technology or strategy by attending an extended seminar or workshop, or by studying systematically a set of books or materials with the help of an expert. Leadership development programs explicitly for presidents in higher education are few compared with opportunities in the corporate world, but offerings of various consulting practices and organizations that focus on leadership can be tailored to meet the needs of a chief executive in higher education. Programs and initiatives sponsored by the national higher education associations in Washington, D.C., are often addressed to the needs of presidents. Sometimes it is helpful for presidents to make organized visits to other campuses, perhaps in the company of other members of their leadership team. Some presidents find renewal by periodically taking a two- or three-month or longer leave to finish a writing or research project, or to study higher education in another culture.

Corporate executives increasingly employ a coach to address persistent issues in interpersonal, behavioral and organizational competencies like communication, negotiation, listening, handling stress, resolving conflict, and so forth. The same process can be used to advantage on campus. A plan will function best if the president can work with several trusted colleagues who are close to the president's work, as well as a coach, to serve as a sounding board and to monitor progress where there are problems and opportunities. This group can be a continuing source of feedback, ideas and suggestions to keep the development process moving forward. Accepting the responsibility of answering to others becomes in itself an ongoing source of motivation and of responsibility.

> A legitimate question can always be raised about whether and how much people can improve their abilities in complex areas like leadership.

A legitimate question can always be raised about whether and how much people can improve their abilities in complex areas like leadership. To be sure, there are many givens of temperament and personality that cannot be altered. But people can change behavior, practices and actions over time more than they believe if they become aware of the issues, feel responsible to answer to a group of colleagues, and can clearly see that making changes will increase personal and professional satisfaction and performance. Persons who are asked to fill the top executive positions in universities usually have demonstrated a large capacity for hard work and high levels of determination. Within the proper framework and with supportive feedback, it is hard to imagine that that same persistence would not be productive in working on personal behavior and practices.

In some cases, even largely positive results will trigger thoughts and plans in many presidents about the longer term direction of their careers. The understanding of the situation that the board gains through the assessment will help it to support the president's career development, to put major decisions into context, and to consider the likelihood and circumstances of a transition, even though one may not occur in the near future.

Closure

Most boards will consider the successful conclusion of the comprehensive assessment an opportunity to reaffirm support for the president and their commitment to a shared set of priorities for the future. The board should use the occasion to inform the campus community of the results of the process, and communicate its gratitude to the many people who participated. After consultation and review by the president, a letter, memorandum or announcement should be sent by the board to the campus community summarizing the process and the general themes and conclusions of the review. The statement provides an opportunity for the board to express its confidence in the president and to suggest broad areas where there are opportunities for improvement going forward. Many of the themes will be familiar ones that the president has already singled out during the evaluation process, and they will not focus on the president alone, but on the work of the institution and the board, as well. In communicating about the process, the president and the board provide a model of openness and of leadership evaluation and development for others on campus to follow.

> **At its best, a comprehensive process contributes to the development of the president's effectiveness and the renewal of his or her commitment to the tasks of leadership.**

At its best, a comprehensive process contributes to the development of the president's effectiveness and the renewal of his or her commitment to the tasks of leadership. It can increase the president's self-understanding and professional satisfaction and set an agenda of plans and actions for the good of the person and the organization. For the board, the process represents the chance to transform a fiduciary responsibility into a collaborative process of leadership. It taps into sources of insight and knowledge about the president's work that enlarge its understanding of the complexities of leadership and the state of the strategic agenda. Its own work becomes more integrated, its influence legitimately enlarged, and its engagement revitalized.

Checklist and Timeline for Comprehensive Assessment

The timeline and actions suggested here assume that there are no major problems in the academic calendar that would make these sequences difficult or impossible. Interviews are hard to arrange with faculty and students during the summer months, and boards are less likely to meet at those times as well. Those realities have to be factored into the timing of the total process.

1. The board defines the purposes and adopts a policy concerning comprehensive presidential reviews to occur every three to four years. **PRIOR ACTION**
2. The chair of the board appoints a small assessment committee of five to six board members, including the president *ex officio*, to take responsibility for the process, under the leadership of the chair or another board member. **WEEK 1**
3. Board passes resolution charging committee to undertake a comprehensive assessment of the president. **WEEK 1**
4. The committee establishes a timeline, resources and staff support for a pending assessment, and decides whether to engage a consultant to assist with the process. Assessment committee chair responsibilities are determined in relation to the work of the board. **WEEK 2**
5. Selection of consultant (if determined a consultant will be engaged). Materials and information are provided to consultant. **WEEK 5**

6. The committee and the president meet with the consultant to discuss the aims of the assessment, questions or focus for interviews, the type of oral and/or written reports that may be desired, and the process to be followed in the interviews. **WEEK 8**

7. President completes self-assessment. **WEEK 10**

8. The staff to the assessment committee, in consultation with the chair, the president and the consultant, develops a schedule of interviews to be held over several days with individuals and small groups. **WEEK 10**

9. The consultant conducts a series of interviews. **WEEKS 12-13**

10. The consultant prepares a report and recommendations for the assessment committee and the board following an agreed oral/and or written format, which is first reviewed with the president. **WEEK 15**

11. The consultant meets with the president, the board chair, the assessment committee and/or the board to present the report. **WEEK 16**

12. The board communicates with the campus about the general results of the assessment and the process that has been followed. **WEEK 16**

13. The president develops ideas and plans for leadership development, and shares its general content with the chair of the board and the assessment committee. **WEEK 18**

Appendix I

Policies and Materials on Presidential Assessment

Governing boards benefit significantly from having policies in place on presidential assessment. The policies give continuity and clarity to the work of the board, provide the president with a clear understanding of the purposes of the process and supply the academic community and key stakeholders with information about how the president's performance is evaluated. The policy should be provided and explained to the president at the time of initial appointment, along with any goals and expectations that have been developed during the search process.

The detailed procedures for annual and comprehensive reviews should be developed in writing by the presidential assessment committee working with the board chair and the president. The foregoing text offers a number of suggestions for relevant procedures, though they should be adapted to the practices and culture of each institution. Other AGB publications referenced previously and listed in the *Sources and References* section of this book offer models of policies and procedures for annual and joint presidential and board assessment. See Merrill Schwartz, *Annual Presidential Performance Reviews*, and Ingram and Weary, *Presidential and Board Assessment in Higher Education.*

Section IA

Illustrative Policy on Annual and Comprehensive Presidential Assessment

Purposes

Assessment provides an appraisal of the president's performance and leadership within the larger goal of contributing to the improvement of the president's and the institution's effectiveness. It accomplishes a variety of related goals, including continuous communication between the board and president about goals and accomplishments, the institution's strategic position and vision, and the effectiveness of organizational decision-making. The process also provides feedback from the board, campus and external stakeholders to increase the president's self-awareness and to bring a focus to his/her plans for professional development. Although not its primary purpose, it provides the board with information concerning compensation and re-appointment decisions, and fulfills various expectations for accountability.

Responsibility

The governing board exercises responsibility for the appointment, support, compensation and evaluation of the president. To that end, the board has adopted the following policy concerning annual and comprehensive assessment.

Principles for Annual Assessment

- The board develops a fair process for annual evaluation that draws on balanced sources of information.
- Annual assessment is ordinarily a private process between the board and the president.
- The board names a committee of several members, including the board chair, to carry out the annual assessment. (A small board may assume this responsibility itself.)
- The core of the process is a written self-assessment by the president.
- Board members who are not on the committee are provided an opportunity to communicate their perspectives.
- After its deliberations, the assessment committee gives the president a chance to respond to the committee's deliberations.
- The chair of the board communicates without delay with the president about the ideas and suggestions resulting from the assessment.
- The chair documents the assessment through a memorandum to the president.
- The president develops a revised set of goals as appropriate, for the institution as well as for professional improvement.
- The president and board agree on goals and priorities for the year ahead.

Principles for Periodic Comprehensive Assessment

- Periodic comprehensive assessment occurs every three to four years and builds on the foundation of annual assessment.
- The assessment should be a formative process, whose primary purpose is enhancing the performance of the president and contributing to his or her professional development.
- The board establishes an assessment committee that includes the chair of the board, the president ex officio, four or five other members, and staff support.

- The committee establishes a timeline and process for confidential interviews on the president's effectiveness and leadership with a significant cross-section of the campus community and external stakeholders.

- The interviews are led by an experienced leader in higher education or a comparable expert, or by a person connected to the campus who can elicit fully objective responses.

- The consultant (or other) reports oral and/or written findings and recommendations to the president, and subsequently to the assessment committee and/or the board. All meetings and materials related to the assessment are confidential.

- With the board's encouragement, the president develops a plan for activities that will improve his or her professional performance, and considers with the board ways to address institutional or board issues that may be part of the assessment findings.

- At the conclusion of the assessment, the board will make a statement to the campus community summarizing the process.

Note: This illustration of board policy for annual and comprehensive presidential review is intended for a public or independent institution that has its own governing board. In the case of a statewide or other multi-campus structure, the system head ordinarily has responsibility for the review of campus heads/presidents, sometimes in conjunction with a local advisory board. See the document in *Appendix II* from the State University of New York (SUNY) that describes the protocols for annual and periodic presidential assessment in a multi-campus system.

Section IB

Sample Letter and Materials for Participants in Comprehensive Assessment

These materials were developed by the author and have been used in several comprehensive presidential assessments.

The sample letter is suggested as an introduction to the purposes of comprehensive presidential evaluation. It is to be provided to interviewees, along with the leadership questions that will guide the interviews. The letter sets a framework that makes the interview process transparent to those participating in it. It would ordinarily be sent with a cover letter from the chair of the board assessment committee a week or so before the meeting. The letter or materials should include a paragraph about the consultant conducting the interviews. Depending on the individual or group being interviewed, it would be accompanied by various forms of information about goals and expectations for the president drawn from prior or current presidential self-assessments, annual reports, or strategic plans and strategic indicators that describe the situation of the institution. The information encourages those being interviewed to place their comments in the context of an interpretation of this information based on their own experience. Board assessment committee chairs and consultants can adapt this sample letter as they choose in communicating with the participants in the interviews.

Sample Letter

Dear Participant:

As many of you are aware, the governing board has adopted a practice that calls for a comprehensive assessment of the president every three to four years to complement the evaluation that occurs annually. The purpose of the process is to contribute ideas and suggestions to improve the effectiveness of the work of the president and of the organization. To accomplish these goals, we are using a process recommended by the Association of Governing Boards of Universities and Colleges (AGB) that includes interviews with various members of the university/college community including faculty, staff, students, alumni, community leaders, political officials, and the governing board. The assessment committee of the board has developed a schedule of interviews that will be conducted by [consultant's name], the former president of [institution's name]. A brief biography of [consultant's name] is included in the enclosed materials. We appreciate deeply your taking the time to meet with [consultant's name] [may include "in a small group meeting"] on [date and time] in [location]. The following description provided by the consultant and the enclosed materials and information will give you a fuller understanding of the goals of a comprehensive assessment. Thank you again for your participation.

Sincerely,

XX

Chair, Assessment Committee

DESCRIPTION OF THE PROCESS TO PARTICIPANTS IN THE INTERVIEWS

As experience suggests and the literature on the topic confirms, the evaluation of leadership is always complex, for the term conveys a number of different meanings in different contexts. As it is exercised in academic organizations, presidential leadership involves the integration of a series of different dimensions of both leadership and management, some of which are in tension with one another. To illustrate: academic decision-making is collegial, administrative authority is hierarchical, and stakeholder relationships are ambiguous and complex. Some of the central strands of presidential leadership relate to the effective and responsible exercise of the formal authority of a position, others to methods, skills and expertise, and yet others to personal qualities and characteristics. As contemporary leadership studies suggest, one of the central motifs implied in all of these forms is the relational or interactive aspect of leadership as a process of influence, direction-setting and sense-making that occurs between leaders and the members of the organization. In many ways, the authority and attributes of academic leaders are assessed by their ability to mobilize the resources and motivate the members of an organization to move in a common direction based on collaborative processes and shared purposes.

Board policy calls for an annual assessment of the president and, every three to four years, a comprehensive presidential assessment. You have been invited to participate in this comprehensive, multi-source evaluation based on confidential small-group and individual interviews with members of the campus community and other stakeholders, conducted by [consultant's name]. None of the comments will be reported in ways that could identify individuals. The consultant intends to assist the board by gathering the perspectives of board members, faculty, staff, alumni, students and community leaders, and others as appropriate. The process will be based on conversations about the *effectiveness* of the work of the president in different contexts of responsibility, as suggested in the questions that follow. The questions are intended to provide a framework for an open conversation that allows participants to clarify and explore issues. The questions have been derived from research and publications on leadership and presidential leadership.

The purpose of the presidential evaluation is to give constructive feedback to the president and provide the governing board with information and insights that help them to meet their responsibilities. The questions and responses are ultimately intended to contribute to a more effective presidency and organization, not to create a check list of successes and failures. The process may also reveal any systemic barriers to effective organizational decision-making and leadership as the consultant pieces together insights gathered across the institution. Although evaluation is the means, the goal of the process is the continuing development of the president's and the institution's capacities to meet its strategic goals. Thus, the board will use the findings to provide feedback to the president on the views of different groups, to enlarge awareness, to provide opportunities for the president to strengthen capabilities and to reorganize processes, priorities and responsibilities as indicated, all in the name of meeting the evolving needs of the institution. The findings of the evaluation also will provide the board and the president with important insights in setting goals for the annual presidential assessment process. Participants are asked to consider these larger developmental and strategic goals of the evaluation.

Participants are also asked to keep in mind that they can be most helpful by providing as much specific evidence and information as possible about the views that they hold. So, the consultant will often ask questions about the source or basis for a particular judgment.

Participants will also be asked to suggest the level or degree of their confidence in a point of view as, for example, in indicating whether their view is strongly held, moderately so, or uncertain.

The consultant will also ask questions about how the president might fulfill his or her responsibilities more effectively, and how things might be done differently by the organization to improve its performance. The consultant will prepare a report for the president, the assessment committee and the board on the findings of the interviews.

Appendix II

Interview Questions and Survey Forms for Annual and Comprehensive Assessment

SECTION IIA

This appendix includes several examples of interview questions and forms concerning presidential performance from existing documents and sources that supplement the examples given in the text.

The first form has been substantially revised and adapted from one used in the past by Moravian College, a liberal arts college in Bethlehem, Pennsylvania. The form could be used by the board committee for annual assessment to gather written opinions from other board members, the administrative leadership team, and faculty leaders on a confidential basis. The form can be modified easily to include other questions to fit the circumstances of each institution.

Annual Presidential Evaluation

The following categories and questions provide a framework for the annual evaluation of the president. Your evaluation should take into consideration the mission and purposes of the college, its charter, the list of board responsibilities and policies on presidential evaluation, and the current strategic plan. Please suggest ways the president and the college can improve their performance.

Questions and Comments	RATING (1–3)

Instructions.
 	
Please enter comments in each section.
 	
Optional: Enter a performance rating for each area, on a scale of 1 to 3. There will be no calculation of averages, but the scale may help to clarify your conclusions.
 	
    Scale:
    3=exceeds expectations
    2=meets expectations
    1=below expectations	

1. Pursuing Our Purposes and Goals Does the president lead the faculty, students and staff to understand the identity, embrace the purposes and realize the goals of the college? Comments:	
2. Strategy Does the president lead an effective strategy process for the college? Has he or she developed initiatives and programs to implement the strategic plan? Comments:	

Questions and Comments	RATING (1–3)
3. Quality of the Academic Program Does the president ensure that the college's academic programs are well-planned, executed, and assessed? Are the college's academic decision-making systems working effectively? Comments:	
4. Generating Resources Do the president and the college obtain sufficient revenues from all fund-raising sources relative to the college's potential? Comments:	
5. Managing Resources Does the president responsibly and efficiently manage the financial and physical resources of the college? Comments:	
6. Managing Key Performance Areas Does the president create a sense of urgency and drive results in key performance areas such as admissions, enrollment, and retention? Comments:	

Questions and Comments	RATING (1–3)
7. Quality of Student Life Does the president foster a quality of student life that promotes the full development of students? Comments:	
8. Representing the Institution Is the president an effective representative of the college? Does he or she maintain productive and influential relationships with important internal and external constituencies? Comments:	
9. Relating to the Board Does the president carry out the board's policies? Does he or she support the board of trustees as it fulfills its governance role? Comments:	
10. Summary What have been the president's major recent achievements in leading the college? Comments: How might the president and the college improve their effectiveness? Comments:	

Section IIB

Questions for Annual Presidential Self-Assessment

The following questions are taken directly, with minor editing, from John Nason's book on presidential assessment, pp. 44–45, as noted in *Sources and References* at the end. Nason, in turn, drew them from an unnamed private college whose trustee committee posed them to the president. They are demanding and penetrating, and they focus on the effort to raise self-awareness and reflect on personal development as well as on accomplishment of strategic priorities and metrics.

1.
   a. Describe your most significant achievements to date. Relate them to your objectives as you perceived them when you accepted your appointment as president.
   b. Describe any difficulties you encountered in achieving these objectives.
   c. Describe modifications you made (if any) in your objectives as originally perceived, the reason(s) for modification, the difficulties encountered in making the modification, and the significant results of the modification.
   d. What aspects of your presidency are the most interesting and rewarding to you? Why?
   e. What aspects of your presidency are the least interesting or most difficult for you? Why?
   f. What would you like to be doing as president that you are not doing now?

2.
   a. What activities have contributed to your personal development since assuming the presidency of the college?
   b. What are your short-term personal development objectives and what plans do you have to accomplish them?
   c. What are your longer range goals?
3. Please express any additional thoughts, desires, ambitions or plans that you have as president of the college.

Section IIC

Illustrative Interview Questions for Comprehensive Assessment

These questions are quoted directly from *Presidential and Board Assessment in Higher Education,* by Richard T. Ingram and William A. Weary (2000) and are intended to be a guide for interviews in a comprehensive presidential and board assessment.

INSTITUTIONAL AGENDA

Reflecting on the president's period of service, how has the institution progressed during this time? What can you point to that indicates the institution's health and standing have been strengthened by virtue of specific institutional goals and priorities having been met? Are any major institutional priorities being neglected?

ACADEMIC LEADERSHIP

How has the institution's general academic standing advanced since the incumbent assumed the presidency? What specific improvements in the quality of the institution's academic programs can be largely attributed to the president's leadership? What other achievements are particularly noteworthy with regard to the president's leadership with the faculty in academic planning and innovation? In enrollment management and admissions?

GENERAL MANAGEMENT AND PLANNING

What can you point to as laudable achievements in the institution's infrastructure, staffing, and information systems? Has the president formed a competent, motivated, and respected management team? Are you aware of improvements in personnel and physical-plant management? How would you describe the way institutional planning is conducted?

FISCAL MANAGEMENT AND BUDGETING

How well does the president understand the institution's financial condition? Has he or she helped the larger community understand it? Has there been success in meeting budgets and containing costs? Reallocating resources? Adhering to good financial (operating and capital) management practices?

FUND RAISING

What successes illustrate the president's ability to raise private dollars from individuals, corporations, and foundations? Is it apparent that the governing board is supportive in its personal philanthropy and related activity? Are donations from alumni steady, increasing, or decreasing? For public institutions: How has the president contributed to the development and success of the institution's endowment or foundation? How effective is the president with the legislature, its key committees, and the governor?

INTERNAL RELATIONSHIPS

With which of the following internal groups has the president been particularly effective and ineffective, and why: the governing board, academic and executive officers, staff, faculty, and students? What advice would you give the president concerning ineffective relationships, if any exist?

EXTERNAL RELATIONSHIPS

With which of the following external groups has the president been particularly effective and ineffective, and why: alumni, local business leaders, elected political leaders, and the media? What advice would you give the president concerning ineffective relationships, if any exist?

DECISION MAKING AND PROBLEM SOLVING

Please describe the president's leadership style. To what extent does he or she delegate decisions when appropriate? How would you gauge the president's ability to cope in crisis situations? Can the president make difficult decisions in timely ways? Does the board encourage the president to demonstrate courageous leadership and to publicly support difficult decisions after they are made? Can you give some explicit examples?

OTHER PERSPECTIVES

Reflecting on the president's years of service, what major achievements or shortcomings come to mind? Is there evidence that the governing board and president are fully supportive of one another? What is the most important thing the president can do to strengthen his or her effectiveness? What is the most important thing the governing board can do to strengthen its effectiveness or the president's effectiveness? Any closing words?

Section IID

10 Questions:
The Craft of Presidential Assessment

These 10 questions on presidential performance have been suggested by Robert Atwell, former president of the American Council on Education, for use in comprehensive presidential assessment. They are found in the article "The Craft of Presidential Assessment," in *Trusteeship* magazine (March/April 2007).

1. **Is the president's vision for the institution consistent with the mission statement, and is that vision shared by the governing board and other stakeholders?** A common disconnect is that the mission statement of a small, public or private institution may refer to serving the local or regional populace, while the president aspires to national research university status. This concept is known as "mission creep," and it can create problems for all types of institutions.

2. **Is the president candid with the board about conflict among or between other stakeholders?** Too many presidents are reluctant to bring troubling or even bad news to the board.

3. **If the board has given the president guidance on what should be his priorities, has the president responded positively to those priorities, or has he ignored or short-changed them?** Are the needs of the institution and the president's priorities compatible, regardless of whether the president and board are in agreement on them? A contemporary reality is that fund raising (from private sources or state legislatures) is the No. 1 priority for most institutions and presidents, and it is the most easily measureable indicator of performance.

4. **If the president is primarily an "outside" president—meaning fund raising, friend-raising, and public relations are top priorities—is that what the board expects? If so, are others in the management team dealing with the "inside" issues?** Presidential responsibilities include fund raising, visioning, human resource management, and financial management, among others. Very few people are equally proficient in all these and other areas.

5. **Are members of the management team "on the same page" with the president and with one another, or are there major areas of conflict or disagreement?** Sometimes a new president from outside the institution inherits an experienced staff that may resist his or her leadership.

6. **Does the president make good personnel appointments, and does he hold his direct reports accountable for achieving results?**

7. **How involved is the president with the formal and informal aspects of faculty governance in such areas as curriculum development and faculty appointment and tenure matters?** Many presidents have concentrated almost exclusively on fund raising and external matters and ignore "inside" issues that are vital to success. Other presidents insist on being involved in all major personnel decisions.

8. **How involved is the president with student-life concerns? Does the president attend student events? Is he or she available to students on a regular or ad hoc basis?**

9. **Does the president provide opportunities for the board to interact with faculty, staff, and students, or does he or she restrict access in the interest of "high control"?**

10. **Is the amount of time the president spends away from the campus appropriate? Is the time spent in the interests of the institution or in the interests of the president's career?**

It should be obvious that the answers to each of these questions will (a) require the reflections of many interviewees and (b) reveal many facets of the institution only indirectly relevant to the president's performance. The part of the assessment most directly related to presidential performance will be successful if it points to areas of needed attention and improvement by all parties.

Section IIE

The list of interview questions here is similar to the one found in the text, but includes a fuller inventory of over 60 items that may be useful for institutions that wish to craft a customized set of questions.

LEADERSHIP CONTEXTS AND QUESTIONS

Strategic Leadership

How effectively does the president:

- Demonstrate an understanding of the culture of the organization and convincingly tell its story?

- Discern and communicate the meaning of external trends and the institution's strategic situation?

- Renew the mission and articulate a compelling vision?

- Shape a productive strategy process and enlist the participation and confidence of others in it?

- Implement the strategy and make things happen to achieve competitive advantage and respond to the driving forces of change and competition?

Educational Leadership

How effectively does the president:

- Propose educational directions and priorities that motivate others?
- Assure academic quality by expecting the use of evidence to improve performance?
- Mobilize resources to support educational programs?
- Encourage and enable educational and curricular change and innovation?
- Understand and participate in academic governance and collaborative decision-making?
- Attract and retain strong faculty?

Organizational Management

How effectively does the president:

- Manage—analyze, organize, plan, direct, evaluate, renew—basic institutional processes and resources (finances, technology, human resources, facilities, services, etc.)?
- Create a sense of urgency and drive results in key performance areas such as admissions, enrollment, retention, student learning, fund raising, research, service, finances and facilities?
- Set high standards and hold people responsible for results?
- Make clear and timely decisions?
- Make tough decisions?
- Use analytical and creative thinking to solve problems?
- Plan for and manage crises?
- Attract, retain and develop talented personnel?
- Build a leadership team and empower and motivate them to achieve beyond their expectations?

Financial Management

How effectively does the president:

- Understand and manage the organization's financial dynamics, metrics and processes (budgeting, costs, revenues, overhead, balances, and investments) and communicate financial realities to stakeholders?
- Manage resources efficiently and build long-term financial equilibrium (create operating balances, add revenues at a faster rate than expenses, provide for depreciation, and increase the purchasing power of the endowment)?
- Inform and engage the board appropriately?

Fund Raising

How effectively does the president:

- Lead and engage others in the fund-raising program?
- Build relationships with major donors?
- Obtain gifts and grants relative to full potential from individuals, alumni, corporations and foundations?
- Provide stewardship for gifts that have been received?
- Inform and engage the board appropriately?

External Relations

How effectively does the president:

- Build credibility and influence with external constituencies?
- Serve the community?
- Provide leadership to local, regional and national higher education?
- Increase the visibility and reputation of the institution?
- Relate to alumni and gain their support?
- Build credibility and influence with the media?
- Influence legislators and public officials?

Internal Relations

How effectively does the president:

- Develop a climate and programs that enhance diversity?
- Interact with students and demonstrate commitment to their welfare?
- Work with the faculty to develop initiatives to advance their work and professional well-being?
- Work with the staff to create opportunities and resources to recognize their service and enhance their development?

Board and Governance Relations

How effectively does the president:

- Build the relationship with the board?
- Gain support from the board, especially on controversial issues?
- Involve and call on the board to facilitate relationships for the president, especially in fund-raising and community relations?
- Develop a good working understanding of the board's, the administration's and the faculty's respective roles in decision making?
- Involve the board in strategy in productive and appropriate ways?
- Focus the board's attention on issues related to the president's professional development and personal welfare?
- Focus the board's attention on decision making and governance systems that need improvement?

Personal Characteristics and Values

How effectively does the president:

- Demonstrate persistence in reaching goals?
- Lead change?
- Use political skills to negotiate agreements, create coalitions and build consensus?

- Display interpersonal and people skills?
- Communicate clearly and convincingly in various forms and contexts?
- Show respect for others?
- Listen?
- Examine and challenge his or her assumptions and show a willingness to explore other viewpoints?
- Understand his or her and others' feelings?
- Reconcile conflict between self and others, and among groups and individuals?
- Demonstrate honesty and integrity?
- Inspire trust and confidence?

Summary Questions

- What have been the president's major accomplishments in the leadership of the institution during the past several years?
- What single thing would you suggest to improve the president's effectiveness?
- What other points need to be covered?

Section IIF

Guidelines for Presidential Reviews and Evaluations at State-Operated Campuses

STATE UNIVERSITY OF NEW YORK (SUNY)

The following guidelines were published for the annual and periodic comprehensive evaluation of the presidents of SUNY campuses. (The list of individual campuses has been omitted.) They illustrate the procedures that are used in one large multi-campus system and offer another example of the topics and questions that are addressed in the evaluation of college and university presidents. (State University of New York, Office of the Chancellor, n.d.)

Overview of Annual Reviews and Formal Evaluations:

The Chancellor of the University has responsibility for the review and evaluation of campus presidents. These Guidelines are designed to be supportive in nature and to allow for regular assessment and reflection by both the President and the Chancellor on the health of the institution and the quality of leadership demonstrated by the President. The Guidelines will be applied in a manner which reflects the unique nature and mission of each State University campus.

Process:

The process shall include two parts: (1) a short annual review of each President; (2) a full scale formal evaluation of all Presidents on a periodic basis.

It is difficult to separate an assessment of a President from an assessment of his/her campus, and therefore, each review conducted under these Guidelines will, to some extent, look both at the overall health of the institution and the quality of the President's stewardship. Usually, the annual review will focus on issues and concerns earlier established by the President and the Chancellor. Thus, each annual review format will reflect factors unique to a particular President and campus. The more formal periodic evaluation will focus on the performance of the President in advancing the mission of the campus within the framework established by the State University. The annual reviews will be performed throughout the year. Formal evaluations will be conducted according to a schedule determined in advance.

Annual Review

I. President's Report to the Chancellor

Every year each President of a state-operated campus shall send a short (three to five pages) report to the Chancellor, with a copy to the Chair of the local College Council for distribution to the Council assessing:

- The overall academic quality of the institution;
- The financial health of the institution;
- Progress made in achieving previously set goals;
- Any institutional or personal problems the President has encountered during the year; and
- The President's goals for the coming year.

II. Chancellor's Review of the Report

The Chancellor shall review the President's report and he/she, or a senior staff member designated by the Chancellor, shall consult with the College Council Chair, College Council, Vice Chancellors, and other sources as appropriate.

III. Meeting between the President and the Chancellor

The President will meet with the Chancellor to review his/her report and other relevant information regarding the President or the campus. The Chancellor and the President will discuss the overall health of the campus and set appropriate goals for the institution and the President for the coming year.

IV. Chancellor's Report to the Board of Trustees

The Chancellor will report, in executive session, to the Board of Trustees on the overall health of the institution and on the progress the President has made in achieving institutional goals.

V. Letter to the President

The yearly review will conclude with a short confidential letter from the Chancellor to the President, outlining the Chancellor's assessment of progress in achieving prior goals, and reiterating the goals set for the coming year. A copy of this letter will be given only to the Board of Trustees and the Chair of the College Council for distribution to the Council.

Formal Evaluation

Each President of a state-operated campus will also be formally evaluated at regular intervals during his/her service. New presidents will be evaluated during their third year of service. It is anticipated that continuing presidents will be formally evaluated every five years, although the Chancellor may institute such an evaluation at a different interval if circumstances deem it appropriate. The purpose of this periodic evaluation will be to assess the President's performance. A broad range of individuals who work closely with the President both on and off campus will be invited by the Chancellor to participate in this evaluation. At the start of the academic year, the Chancellor will provide to the Board of Trustees, in public session, a list of Presidents undergoing a formal evaluation.

I. President's Report to the Chancellor

The President shall submit a self-evaluation report to the Chancellor assessing the state of the institution and his/her stewardship thereof. This report should address the following issues:

1. The overall academic quality of the institution, including:
    a. The quality of academic programs, including the general education program, undergraduate programs, and graduate programs where applicable;
    b. The quality of faculty appointments, recruitment and retention;
    c. The success of the institution's student recruitment and retention strategies;
    d. Significant changes, either proposed or implemented, in academic programs;
    e. Student outcomes, including any measures that the campus employs to ensure that appropriate learning is taking place in the subject and skill areas covered by their undergraduate and graduate programs; and
    f. The President's role in building and/or maintaining academic strength.
2. The financial health of the institution, including:
    a. How allocated resources have been utilized;
    b. Financial planning for the institution's future needs;
    c. The President's fund-raising record and future development plans;
    d. The institution's record of attracting external funds for research.
3. The institution's record of service to its local area and to the State.
4. The President's record representing the institution and articulating its goals to a variety of external constituencies (alumni, parents, local and state legislators, and community leaders) and to internal constituencies (students; faculty and staff).
5. The President's record of service to SUNY, the community in which the campus is located, and to regional and/or national educational associations.

6. The condition of the physical plant and plans for future building and/or renovation.

7. Special challenges that the institution or the President have faced since the last performance review.

8. Overall campus morale.

II. Appointment of Evaluation Team

The Chancellor will appoint a team to conduct the formal evaluation and to make a confidential assessment of the President's performance. This team will consist of one external peer evaluator (a current or former President of a non-SUNY institution of similar size and character, or another recognized leader in public higher education), and may also include a senior academic administrator or senior faculty member, and a senior member of the System Administration. In appointing the team, the Chancellor will consult with the President about potential evaluators in order to avoid any bias or conflicts of interest.

III. Comments on Presidential Stewardship and the Institution

A.   Presidential Stewardship

The Chancellor will invite members of the College Council, the College Foundation Board, faculty governance leaders, student government leaders, as well as representatives of the alumni association and the professional and support staffs to submit written comments on the quality of the President's stewardship. The Chancellor will also seek input from the Vice Chancellors and senior system administrators as appropriate. Requests for comments regarding Presidential stewardship shall be considered confidential.

B.   The Institution

The Chancellor may request comment from other interested parties, including the public, concerning the institution and their knowledge of matters concerning the institution. When requesting such comment, the Chancellor will make it clear that the evaluation is a routine, periodic evaluation and does not necessarily reflect a loss of confidence by the Chancellor or others in the President's stewardship of the institution. Comments from such other interested parties may be considered by the Chancellor in the Presidential review if such matters are, within the judgment of the Chancellor, deemed appropriate and relevant and where based on the direct, first-hand knowledge of the person commenting.

IV. Campus Visit by the Evaluation Team

After reviewing the President's report, background information about the institution, and the written comments solicited from the individuals and groups described above, the evaluation team will visit the campus to meet the President. The team may also meet with representatives of appropriate constituency groups, including members of the College Council, the campus Foundation, senior administrators, faculty, students, and staff. The President will be consulted as to the timing and organization of the campus visit. At the end of their visit, the team will meet privately with the President to share their views on the overall health of the institution and the quality of the President's leadership.

V. Report from the Team to the Chancellor

After visiting the campus, the team will consult with the Chancellor regarding its findings, and prepare and submit a written report on the quality of the President's stewardship. The report may include suggested future goals for the President. This report is considered to be intra-agency material, non-final and prepared to assist the Chancellor and the Board of Trustees in its deliberative process of evaluating the job performance of the President. The report is considered a confidential, personnel matter, to be shared only with the Board of Trustees in executive session.

VI. Chancellor's Report to the Board of Trustees

After consulting with the President regarding the contents of the report, the Chancellor will report, in executive session, to the Board of Trustees on the conclusions of the evaluation team, and offer his own assessment of the President's performance.

VII. Final Report

The evaluation will conclude with a short confidential letter or report from the Chancellor to the President outlining the Chancellor's assessment of the President's performance. A copy will be shared with the Board of Trustees and the College Council Chair for distribution to the Council.

Sources and References

Association of Governing Boards of Universities and Colleges. *The Leadership Imperative*. Washington, D.C.: AGB, 2006.

Association of Governing Boards of Universities and Colleges. "Statement on Board Accountability." Washington, D.C.: AGB, 2007.

Atwell, Robert E. "The Craft of Presidential Assessment," *Trusteeship*, (March/April 2007), pp. 28-32.

Atwell, Robert H. and Jane V. Wellman. *Presidential Compensation in Higher Education*. Washington, D.C.: Association of Governing Boards of Universities and Colleges, 2000.

Bolman, L. G., and T. Deal. *Reframing Organizations*. San Francisco: Jossey-Bass, 2003.

Fisher, J. and Martha W. Tack. The *Effective College President*. Bowling Green, OH: Bowling Green University, 1988.

Fisher, J. and James V. Koch. *Presidential Leadership: Making a Difference*. Phoenix, AZ: Oryz, 1996.

Fletcher, Clive. *Appraisal, Feedback and Development: Making Performance Review Work*. Abingdon, OX: Routledge, 2008.

Kaplan, Robert E., and Robert B. Kaiser. "Stop Overdoing Your Strengths," Harvard Business Review (February 2007), pp. 1-6.

Kaufmann, Joseph. "Supporting the President and Assessing the Presidency." In R.T. Ingram, (Ed.), *Governing Public Colleges and Universities*, (pp. 126-146), San Francisco: Jossey-Bass, (1993).

Kerr, C. and Marian L. Gade. *The Many Lives of Academic Presidents: Time, Place and Character*. Washington, D.C.: AGB, 1986.

Ingram, Richard T. and William Weary. *Presidential and Board Assessment in Higher Education*. Washington, D.C.: AGB, 2000.

Longenecker, Clinton O. and Dennis A. Gioia. "The Executive Appraisal Paradox." Academy of Management Executive, 6 (2) 1992, pp.18-28.

Moore, John W. and Joanne M. Burrows. "Presidential Succession and Transition: Beginning, Ending, and Beginning Again." Washington, D.C.: American Association of State Colleges and Universities, 2001.

Morrill, Richard L. *Strategic Leadership in Academic Affairs: Clarifying the Board's Responsibilities*. Washington, D.C.: AGB, 2002.

Morrill, Richard L. *Strategic Leadership: Integrating Strategy and Leadership in Colleges and Universities*. Westport, CT: ACE/Praeger, 2007.

Nason, John. *Board Assessment: A Guide to the Periodic Review of the Performance of Chief Executives*. Washington, D.C.: AGB, 1984.

Schwartz, Merrill P. *Assessing the Performance of Academic Presidents*. Ph.D. Dissertation. University of Maryland, College Park, 1998.

Schwartz, Merrill P. "A National Survey of Presidential Performance Assessment Policies and Practices: AGB Occasional Paper No. 34." Washington, D.C.: AGB, 1998.

Schwartz, Merrill P. "AGB Board Basics: Annual Presidential Performance Reviews." Washington, D.C.: AGB, 2001.

Tranquada, Robert E. "The Compensation Committee." Board Basics Series. Washington, D.C.: AGB, 2001.

About the Author

Richard L. Morrill is chancellor of the University of Richmond, a position that he assumed in 1998 to serve as an ambassador of good will following his 10-year presidency. In 2009 he was also named president of the Teagle Foundation in New York City.

On his retirement from the Richmond presidency, he was named to the Distinguished University Chair in Ethics and Democratic Values that carries his name, from which he retired in 2004. Prior to his association with the University of Richmond, Morrill served as president of Centre College from 1982 to 1988 and as president of Salem College from 1979 to 1982. He was chief of staff to the provost of Pennsylvania State University from 1977 to 1979, and held a variety of faculty and administrative positions at Chatham College from 1968-1977.

Morrill received his A.B. in History, *magna cum laude*, from Brown University in 1961, his B.D. in 1964 from Yale University, where he was a Woodrow Wilson Fellow, and his Ph.D. in religion from Duke University, where he was a James B. Duke Fellow. He is a member of *Phi Beta Kappa* and has received honorary degrees from four institutions, including the *École des Hautes Etudes Internationales* in Paris, France. He is also a member of the Order of Academic Palms and the Order of National Merit of the French Republic. The Commission on Colleges of the Southern Association of Colleges and Schools awarded him its Distinguished Leadership Award in 2008.

Morrill currently is president of the board of the Richmond Symphony Foundation, a director of the Library of Virginia Foundation, and of two corporations. Previously he was chairman of the board of ChildFund International. He also served as treasurer of the Association of American Colleges and Universities (AAC&U), director of the National Association of Independent Colleges and Universities (NAICU), president of the Southern Association of Colleges and Schools (SACS), chairman of the College Commission of SACS, and as a member of two commissions of the American Council on Education (ACE). He has worked closely with AGB on a variety of projects and programs on presidential and board assessment.

Morrill has written and spoken widely on issues of values and ethics in liberal education and has published several articles and made numerous presentations on strategic planning and leadership for colleges and universities. He is the author of *Teaching Values in College: Facilitating Ethical, Moral and Value Awareness in Students* (Jossey-Bass, 1980), *Strategic Leadership in Academic Affairs: Clarifying the Board's Responsibilities* (AGB, 2002), and *Strategic Leadership: Integrating Strategy and Leadership in Colleges and Universities* (ACE/Praeger, 2007).

Notes

1 Association of Governing Boards of Universities and Colleges, "Higher Education Governance Survey," (Washington, D.C.: AGB, 2008).

2 Schwartz, Merrill P. *Assessing the Performance of Academic Presidents*, Ph.D. Dissertation. University of Maryland, College Park, 1998.

3 Association of Governing Boards of Universities and Colleges, *Strategic Imperatives: New Priorities for Higher Education*, (Washington, D.C.: AGB, 2009) p. 14.

4 Paul Fain, "American U. Faces a Tussle at the Top," The Chronicle of Higher Education, October 7, 2005.

5 Raymond F. Cotton, "Firing the President," *The Chronicle of Higher Education*, March 11, 2006.

6 Association of Governing Boards of Universities and Colleges, *The Leadership Imperative*. (Washington, D.C.: AGB, 2006). The Association of Governing Boards of Universities and Colleges. "Statement on Board Accountability," (Washington, D.C.: AGB, 2006).

7 For a discussion of the issues in the 1970s, reflecting a period of intense campus activism, see John Nason, *Presidential Assessment: A Guide to the Periodic Review of the Performance of Chief Executives*, Washington, D.C.: AGB, 1980. See also James Fisher and M. Tack, The *Effective College President* (OH: Bowling Green University, 1988); Joseph Kaufmann, "Supporting the President and Assessing the Presidency" in R.T. Ingram, (Ed.), *Governing Public Colleges and Universities* (San Francisco: Jossey-Bass, 1993); Clark Kerr and Miriam Gade, *The Many Lives of Academic Presidents: Time, Place and Character* (Washington, D.C.: AGB, 1986); Richard T. Ingram and William A. Weary, *Presidential and Board Assessment in Higher Education* (Washington, D.C.: AGB, 2000).

8 John Nason, *Presidential Assessment: A Guide to the Periodic Review of the Performance of Chief Executives*, (Washington, D.C.: AGB, 1980).

[9] Merrill Schwartz, *Annual Presidential Performance Reviews*, (Washington, D.C.: AGB, 2001).

[10] Ingram and Weary, *op.cit.* p.19.

[11] Schwartz, *op cit.*

[12] James MacGregor Burns, *Transforming Leadership: A New Pursuit of Happiness*, (New York: The Atlantic Monthly Press, 2003) p. 185.

[13] AGB, *The Leadership Imperative*, *op. cit.* p.34.

[14] Nason, *op. cit.* p.17.

[15] Association of Governing Boards of Universities and Colleges, *Renewing the Academic Presidency: Stronger Leadership for Tougher Times*. (Washington, D.C.: AGB, 1996) p.9.

[16] Burton R Clark, *The Academic Life: Small Worlds, Different Worlds*. (Princeton, N.J: Carnegie Foundation for the Advancement of Teaching, 1987) p. 274.

[17] Richard Morrill, *Strategic Leadership: Integrating Strategy and Leadership in Colleges and Universities*. (Westport, CT: ACE/Praeger, 2007).

[18] AGB, *The Leadership Imperative. op. cit.*, p. 9.

[19] Jim Collins, *Good to Great: Why Some Companies Make the Leap and Others Don't*. (New York: Harper, Collins, 2001) p. 74.

[20] Schwartz, *Annual Presidential Reviews*, op. cit.

[21] *Ibid.*

[22] *Ibid.*, p. 3.

[23] *Ibid.*, p. 3.

[24] *Ibid.*, p. 13.

[25] Nason, *op. cit.*, pp 44–45.

[26] *Ibid.*, pp. 11–12.

[27] This hypothetical case study and the one at the end of Chapter IV were developed by Kenneth Shaw, former president of Syracuse University, and edited by the author. They have been used in a similar form in workshops on presidential assessment sponsored by AGB.

[28] Robert E. Atwell, "The Craft of Presidential Assessment," *Trusteeship*. March/April, 2007, pp. 28-32.

[29] For a useful perspective on balancing leadership strengths that has influenced this discussion, see Robert E. Kaplan and Robert B. Kaiser, "Stop Overdoing Your Strengths," *Harvard Business Review*, February, 2009.

[30] Clive Fletcher, *Appraisal, Feedback and Development: Making Performance Review Work*, (Abingdon, OX: Routledge, 2008).

[31] These orientations or frames of leadership are adapted from ones developed by Lee Bolman and Terry Deal in *Reframing Organizations*, (San Francisco: Jossey-Bass, 2003).

[32] www.Decision-Wise.com. 9/21/2007.

[33] Marshall Goldsmith, *What Got You Here Won't Get You There: How Successful People Become Even More Successful*, (New York: Hyperion, 2007) pp. 41–42.